MARIA RITA SAULLE

NATO AND ITS ACTIVITIES

A political and juridical approach
on consultation

Preface
by
EMILIO COLOMBO
President of the European Parliament

1979
OCEANA PUBLICATIONS, INC.
DOBBS FERRY, NEW YORK

Library of Congress Catalog Card No. 78-68924

Tip. F. Centenari - Roma
Finito di stampare il 31-1-1979

CONTENTS

6

ANNEXES

7

PREFACE

Thirty years ago the democratic countries of the West signed the North Atlantic Treaty and the organization which emerged as a result was a military alliance with the aim of mutual defence of its members.

The changes which took place in international relations in that period and, in particular, the evolution in the international balance from a bipolar to a multipolar system have carried political cooperation to a position of ever growing importance among the activities of the Alliance.

Consultation between the member States, as a consequence, assumed a very important role in the functions of the Alliance and has increased continuously in this latter period, due particularly to the Three Wise Men's Report, contributions to the draft of which were made by On. Gaetano Martino, at that time Italian Minister of Foreign Affairs.

As a firm supporter of the ideal of a United Europe, I am very happy to be able to say that consultation has also helped to create a better understanding and balance between the two sides of the Atlantic. Since political cooperation among the member countries of the European Community began in October 1970, consultation in NATO has provided a convenient means for the Nine to compare their own positions with those of their allies and especially with that of the United States.

Many differences between members have been settled by means of political consultation and closer cooperation has been established in the political, economic, financial, scientific and juridical fields.

Nowadays, all events affecting international policy, in whichever part of the world they may occur, constitute a subject for consultation by NATO's members. Through consultation a high degree of coordination has been realized between NATO, other international and supranational organizations in the political, economic, financial, scientific and juridical fields.

This study, carried out by Maria Rita Saulle, Professor of the History of Treaties and International Policy at the Faculty of Law of the University of Rome, considers all the most important results of consultation among NATO's members and indicates the juridical and political values of this system of cooperation.

EMILIO COLOMBO
President of the European Parliament

ACKNOWLEDGMENTS

This book is published with the aid of a contribution from NATO and I wish to thank Dr. Fernand Welter, Head, Education and Cultural Relations, NATO, for his guidance.

I am very grateful to the staff of the NATO Defense College for their help in the research for this study. Special thanks to miss Jane Tagford for valuable and continous assistance.

INTRODUCTION

When, on the fourth day of April 1949, twelve States from Europe and North America, all bordering on, or connected in some way with the Atlantic Ocean, signed the North Atlantic Treaty, the cold war between the Soviet Union and the United States was escalating. However this tension was not recent, it was already perceptible before the end of the Second World War, at the Yalta Conference in February 1945. At that time there were many discussions concerning the division of Germany and reparation for war damages, the government of Poland, the Polish borders and the French position in the occupation of Germany.

The tension grew and became deeper at the Potsdam Conference in July 1945, when the United States and the United Kingdom, on one side, and the Soviet Union, on the other, discussed their positions, especially with regard to Bulgaria, Rumania and Greece, without reaching any agreement. There was also disagreement about the Russian requests to obtain the trusteeship administration of Libya and control of the Straits of the Bosphorus and the Dardanelles.

Disagreement arose again at the Conference of Foreign Ministers held in London in September 1945. The United Kingdom proposed that an impartial enquiry should be opened in order to examine the situation of Bulgaria and Rumania the proposal was blocked by the intervention of Mr. Molotov Foreign Minister of the Soviet Union.

The impossibility of reaching agreement on the main problems of foreign policy was confirmed at the Peace Conference, opened in Paris on July 29, 1946. The contents of the peace treaties with Italy, Finland, Bulgaria, Hungary and Rumania were decided at the Conference, but due to the difficulties in reaching an agreement, the treaties were not signed until February 10, 1947.

During the period 1947 to 1949, relations between the two Powers deteriorated even further. At a meeting held in Moscow in March 1947, the Foreign Ministers were unable to decide Germany's fate and another Conference of Foreign Ministers, held in London in November 1947, named the « Conference of last possibility », during which the participants discussed the Saar situation, Germany's borders and a peace treaty with Austria, demonstrated how strict and incompatible were the positions of the United States and the Soviet Union.

The Foreign Ministers' meeting held in Paris in May 1949, to discuss the situation of Germany and Austria, did not reach any conclusion other than establish a « modus vivendi » on Berlin, which had already been divided into two sectors. All cooperation, that had developed between the United States, the Soviet Union and the United Kingdom during the war, came to an end in 1948, with the « Nazi-Soviet Relations » disclosure in which the ties of friendship between Germany and the Soviet Union at the start of the Second World War were made known. At that time the doctrine of peaceful coexistence between the two Powers was a long way off.

There were many other factors which made relations between the United States and the Soviet Union worse, e.g., in 1947, when the Security Council of the United Nations established, by means of a commission of enquiry, that Albania and Bulgaria were responsible for the incidents which had occurred in Greece, all draft resolutions, recommending United Nations action, were blocked by the veto of the Soviet Union. The same happened with the admission of Italy to the United Nations.

The pressure exercised by the Soviet Union, especially in Rumania, Bulgaria and Poland, was in a certain way balanced in the field of international relations by the economic and military aid offered by the United States, following the « Truman doctrine » of March 1947, to European countries « resisting attempted subjugation by armed minorities, or by outside pressure ».

The « Truman doctrine » should be taken into account when evaluating the Vandenberg Resolution of April 28, 1948. Senator Vandenberg, in consultation with the State Department, and in the light of the Brussels Treaty of March 17, 1948, which grouped Belgium, France, Luxembourg, the Netherlands and the United Kingdom together with the aim of creating the Western European Union, presented this Resolution to the United States Senate: it was adopted on June 11, 1948. The Resolution allowed the United States to associate « by constitutional process, with such regional and other collective arrangements as are based on continuous and effective self-help and mutual aid ». The principal aim of this association was to make a « contribution to the maintenance of peace » by means of the exercise of « the right of individual or collective self-defence under Article 51 (of the United Nations Charter) » in case of any armed attack « affecting its national security ».

In the Summer of 1948 Senator Vandenberg's idea of joining the Brussels Treaty States with Canada and the United States started taking shape and in March 1949 a draft treaty was prepared. On April 4, 1949, the United Kingdom, France, Belgium, the Netherlands, Luxembourg, the United States, Canada, Italy, Denmark, Iceland, Norway and Portugal signed the North Atlantic Treaty, which was ratified by these countries five months later.

Greece and Turkey acceded to the Treaty on February 8, 1952, and the Federal Republic of Germany became a member of the Organization on May 9, 1955.

The North Atlantic Treaty consists of fourteen articles in which reference to the United Nations Charter is frequently made, as will be demonstrated in the following pages.

Even though the Treaty reaffirms the necessity for the mutual defence of its members and was concluded during a period of cold war escalation, it cannot be considered solely a military agreement, since it proclaims the importance of economic and social progress and affirms, within the framework of the United Nations Charter, the necessity for cooperation among the members of the Alliance in political, economic, social and cultural fields.

Following precisely the same lines as the United Nations Charter, the North Atlantic Treaty affirms the necessity for the settlement of any international dispute by peaceful means and the maintenance of international peace, security and justice.

The Treaty, in common with the Charter, also aims at contributing to peaceful and friendly international relations by strengthening the free institutions of the members through bringing about a better understanding of the principles upon which these institutions are founded and by promoting conditions of stability and well-being.

The Treaty is linked with the Charter both by the provisions regarding collective self-defence (Article 51), in accordance with the Vandenberg Resolution, and by the provisions concerning regional arrangements appearing in

Chapter VIII of the Charter. The North Atlantic Treaty is, in fact, a regional arrangement (¹).

In the North Atlantic Alliance, as in any other alliance, the relationship between members calls for a regular exchange of information on events of interest to the Alliance as a whole. This exchange of information covers all fields and is the only means by which an alliance can function.

An exchange of views is necessary before taking a decision (²) and this system of cooperation enables the members of the union of States, which is what an alliance is, to appear united and in a position to take decisions as a whole. This system of cooperation is very useful in the

---

(¹) The opinion that the North Atlantic Treaty should be considered a regional arrangement and the North Atlantic Treaty Organization as a regional organization or agency, has given rise to many perplexities in the field of international law doctrine. See, on this subject, VAN KLEFFENS, *Regionalism in Political Pacts with Special Reference to the North Atlantic Treaty*, in the *American Journal of International Law*, 1949, p. 665; NISOT, *Le Traité de l'Atlantique-Nord et la Charte des Nations Unies*, in the *Revue de droit comparé*, 1951, p. 145; SERENI, *Diritto internazionale*, II, Section II, Milan 1960, p. 1221.

This question has not only a theoretical, but a practical importance because, if the North Atlantic Treaty is considered a regional arrangement, the Security Council of the United Nations shall, where appropriate, utilize it for enforcement action under its authority on the basis of Article 53 of the Charter. But, according to Article 53, no enforcement action shall be taken under regional arrangements or by regional agencies without the authorization of the Security Council. It is clear that if NATO is considered a regional agency in the sense of Chapter VIII of the Charter of the United Nations, any Permanent Member of the Security Council could paralyze the enforcement action by means of a negative vote.

(²) See NATO *Facts and Figures*, Brussels, 1976, p. 97. See also Chapter III of this study.

military, judicial and political fields. On the military side, it is essential that members have the same ideas on and concept of the main military problems and their solution. It is equally necessary, on the political side, that governments exchange views before deciding on their conduct with other States and organizations.

In every case mentioned here, cooperation may involve both political and juridical consultation (3). In fact, all the activities of the Alliance connected in any way with the various aims of the United Nations, as stated in the Charter, involve political and juridical consultation among the members of NATO and between NATO and other bodies of the international community.

Cooperation and coordination among members is mentioned many times in the provisions of the Charter quoted by the Treaty and where there is no specific reference, the Articles of the Treaty are worded in such a way that compliance involves cooperation or coordination in both the political and the juridical fields.

In certain cases the importance of the problem facing the Alliance regarding the interpretation and execution of these provisions may be so significant that the system of consultation and cooperation in the political and juridi-

---

(3) Consultation is also referred to in this sense by SCHAUS, *Le Conseil de l'Atlantique Nord, son fondement et ses structures, ses compétences et ses missions,* in *Chronique de Politique étrangère,* 1971, vol. XXII, No. 3, pp. 378-379.

Consultation has also entered the field of technology and its importance in this sphere was stressed by the Italian Government in 1966. Consequently, at the meeting of the North Atlantic Council, held in Paris from December 15-16, 1966, the Ministers adopted a Resolution in which they invited the Permanent Representatives to study a procedure for the examination and implementation of the Italian proposals. NATO *Final Communiqués,* pp. 181-183.

cal fields cannot be limited to the exchange of information relating to events among the members, but must be extended to other States and organizations outside the Alliance. The reason for this is that the solution of a particular problem may require either the participation or the cooperation of States or organizations from other areas of the world, or call for the contribution of a maximum number of States or organizations. In such cases the Alliance has to contact foreign States and organizations in order to achieve an identity of view among as large a number of States as possible.

CHAPTER I

Rules Regarding Consultation

1. *Rules Involving Consultation*

The consultation system for the juridical and political fields of the North Atlantic Alliance is based on: 1) provisions of treaty that implicitly or explicitly require such a system; 2) provisions of other treaties concluded by members of the Alliance or by the Alliance as a whole; 3) provisions created by organs of the Alliance or by Committees of its organs, which have indicated this as the most useful and productive system for realizing the various aims of the Alliance (¹).

Apart from the last provision, which will be discussed later since its determination and interpretation is strictly connected with the organ's activity in the sphere of political and juridical consultation, this Chapter will be devoted to the examination of the provisions of the Treaty relating to the consultation system and to that of the rules contained in other treaties concluded by or concerning the Alliance.

(¹) See Chapter III, para. 1.

2. *Rules of the North Atlantic Treaty Implicitly Requiring Consultation.*

Some of the rules of the North Atlantic Treaty implicitly require a system of consultation between members. These rules appear in Articles 1, 2, 3, 5 and 10 of the Treaty, which establish the rights and obligations of all Parties to the Treaty. For this reason, none of these rules mentions a Party or a member of the organization, they all indicate the « Parties », i.e., the members are obliged to adhere to a certain pattern of behaviour.

Some of these rules are closely connected with the Charter of the United Nations; in Articles 1, 2, 3 and 5 there is express reference to the Charter.

Article 1 relates to the settlement of any international dispute in which the Parties may be involved by peaceful means. This Article also establishes that the Parties are obliged to refrain, in international relations, from the threat or use of force in any manner inconsistent with the purposes of the United Nations [2].

It is clear that the settlement of a dispute calls for consultation between the Parties involved. These consultations may either be of a juridical or political nature depending on whether the subject of the dispute is the determination, the application or the interpretation of an international law (OR THE INTERPRETATION OF AN ARTICLE OF INTERNATIONAL LAW), or whether it is a political question. In the first case, however, a certain

---

[2] See, on the application of Article 1, the Resolution (of Dec. 1956) on the Peaceful Settlement of Disputes and Differences between Members of the North Atlantic Treaty Organization, in **NATO** *Final Communiqués,* 1949-1974, p. 103.

juridical solution may be chosen for political reasons and would have been preceded by political consultation.

The above also applies to the second obligation contained in Article 1: the refusal of force in international relations. When it constitutes an obligation for one or more members of an organization, it eventually requires the assent of all members, because one member's conduct towards States outside the Organization may not be compatible with that of the other members; for example, if a member refuses to agree to the use of force against a State outside the Organization and the other members disagree with this decision, it might result in the member States acting at variance with one another. In order to avoid this, the members would consult each other on the advisability of accepting the refusal in that particular case. Consultations of this kind would obviously pay special attention to the political factors — the political, geographical and strategic situation of the country which refuses to agree to the use of force, its importance in the Alliance and the political situation of the country against which they wish to use force. Whatever the outcome of these discussions, the object of consultation is to give the Organization a unified policy, harmonizing the policies of all the member States.

It is not by chance that the United Nations Organization entrusts the settlement of international disputes to a collegial organ, the Security Council, which groups a certain number of members together and only functions and operates in this respect with the agreement of a special majority of the members. As the North Atlantic Organization does not have an organ similar to the Security Council, disputes are settled by the Parties concerned through the consultation system.

The realization of the principle contained in Article 2 also requires consultation among the members of the North Atlantic Treaty Organization. This Article indicates that an important duty of the Parties is contribution « toward the further development of peaceful and friendly international relations by strengthening their free institutions ». Another obligation mentioned in this Article is the elimination of conflict from economic policies and the encouragement of economic collaboration between any or all Parties.

The elimination of conflict necessarily involves consultation, since a conflict needs, by its very definition, at least two parties, one of which questions the pretensions of the other. For this reason, its elimination needs the collaboration of at least two parties. Since « economic collaboration » is concerned, it is similarly clear that it can only be realized by means of consultations among the Parties to the Treaty in the economic and political fields. The link between economy and politics is, indeed, very strong as some of the decisions taken in the economic field are prepared and decided by the political organs of the States; and some of the political decisions are dictated by the economic situation of those countries.

Even though Article 3 appears at first sight to contain a rule concerning solely the military aspects of the Alliance, it can be quoted for the purpose of political and juridical consultation, because its meaning and interpretation indicate that the capacity of resistance to an armed attack is maintained and developed for the Parties, separately and jointly, by means of continuous and effective self-help and mutual aid. Mutual aid obviously requires consultation among the Parties, implying, of course, evaluation of a military character; but at the same time it involves considerations of a political nature, since the aid can be granted or denied for political reasons.

Article 5 contains a rule indicating that use of the consultation system is necessary, even though it would be very complicated. The qualification of an armed attack against one or more of the Parties as an attack against them all requires an evaluation by all Parties of the situation arising from such an attack. This means that they must initially decide whether an attack should be considered of the kind indicated by Article 5, i.e., implying military intervention by all Parties. This decision would be taken on the basis of political consultation as political reasons may induce the Parties to limit the area of conflict and try to find a solution to the problem by peaceful means instead of putting into action the mechanism foreseen by Article 5. Article 51 of the Charter of the United Treaty, in recognizing the right of individual or collective self-defence, requires, should a case such as that indicated by Article 5 occur, consultation among the Parties.

Collective self-defence, as detailed in Article 51 of the Charter, needs agreement between all participating States; and such agreement can be reached by means of political consultation. It is, in fact, on the basis of political considerations that one or more States may decide to undertake an action of collective self-defence.

It should also be mentioned that Article 5 of the North Atlantic Treaty expressly establishes that the assistance given by Parties to the Party or Parties attacked can be decided and acted upon « individually and in concert with the other Parties ». The expression « in concert with... » clearly means that the uniformity of political action can be reached by means of continuous relations, rather than continuous consultation among members of the Alliance.

According to Article 10 of the Treaty « unanimous agreement » among Parties is also necessary when any other European State in a position to further the principles of the Treaty and to contribute to the security of the North Atlantic area is invited to accede to the Treaty. This Article constitutes the accession (or adhesion) clause. With reference to this, it should be mentioned that the admission of a State to the Alliance is considered possible only after members have verified, by means of consultation, that the State is in a position to carry out the duties deriving from membership of the Treaty and is, in particular, in a position to contribute to the security of the North Atlantic area and further the principles of the Treaty.

The mechanism for accession to the Treaty is very like that for admission to the United Nations as stipulated in Article 4 of the UN Charter. Accession to the Treaty is, in common with that to the United Nations, entirely discretionary [3]. This mechanism allows States other than those bordering on or connected in some way with the Atlantic Ocean to become members of the North Atlantic Treaty Organization.

3. *North Atlantic Treaty Rules Explicitly Requiring Consultation*

Article 4 of the North Atlantic Treaty explicitly requires a system of consultation. It states that: « the Parties will consult together whenever, in the opinion of any of them, the territorial integrity, political independence or security

---

[3] See, on this problem, MORELLI, *Nozioni di diritto internazionale pubblico*, Padova, p. 313 (seventh edition, 1967).

of any of the Parties is threatened ». On the basis of this Article, the main implement for both the prevention and the settlement of international conflicts is the consultation system. In fact, since the conclusion of the Treaty there have been many instances in which political independence or security and territorial integrity have endangered world peace, for example the Berlin crisis, the use of nuclear weapons, the Hungarian revolution and its suppression, the Cuba blockade etc., all events which endangered or might have endangered the political independence and territorial integrity of one or more of the Parties.

4. *Rules Implying Consultation Inserted in Agreements Concluded by the Alliance or by its Members.*

There are many agreements, concluded either by the North Atlantic Treaty Organization as a whole, or by individual members of the Alliance in order to achieve the aims of the Treaty, containing rules which involve a system of consultation among members. In this connection, mention may first be made of the agreement between the Parties to the North Atlantic Treaty regarding the status of their forces which was signed in London on June 19, 1951. Articles XVI and XVII of this agreement contain provisions implying a complex system of consultation.

Article XVI lays down that « all differences between the contracting Parties relating to the interpretation or application of this Agreement shall be settled by negotiation between them without recourse to any outside jurisdiction. Except where express provision is made to the contrary in this Agreement, differences which cannot be settled by direct negotiation shall be referred to the North Atlantic Council ».

The meaning of this rule is clear: if there are any differences between the Parties relating to a matter of interpretation or of application of the agreement, the contracting Parties should settle their disputes by means of negotiation, i.e., by means of consultation among themselves. These consultations will either have a juridical or a political character depending on whether the subject of the difference is juridical or political. For example, a difference on the interpretation of a provision of the agreement is highly likely to have a juridical content and therefore to be a juridical difference. However, settlement may also involve political evaluations requiring political consultation, because the choice of one interpretation rather than another may be suggested by political considerations.

On the other hand, a difference on the application of the agreement has a much higher probability of being of a political character from the beginning and of being settled on the basis of political evaluations. It cannot, however, be excluded that the solution of the dispute may be of a juridical nature if it is reached through considerations founded on the rules of the Treaty, or on other international rules.

This opinion is also confirmed by the fact that Article XVI refers differences, which cannot be settled by direct negotiation, to the North Atlantic Council. In fact, as will be mentioned later, the North Atlantic Council is the principal organ of the North Atlantic Treaty Organization (⁴)

(⁴) See Chapter III, para. 2.

responsible for consultation. The Council, after an opportune examination of the question, will either propose a solution for the differences, in which case it may so happen that the Council's proposals are the result of previous consultations between the Parties in the juridical or political fields, or will invite the Parties to consult each other in order to find a way of settling the dispute.

Article XVII of the Status of Forces Agreement lays down that: « any contracting Party may at any time request the revision of any article of this agreement. The request shall be addressed to the North Atlantic Council ».

Treaty revision constitutes one of the most important political problems in international relations. The revision can be put into effect as soon as the parties to a treaty have reached agreement both on the advisability of revising a certain provision and on the modification to be made to the provision. It is clear that, at these two moments in the revision process, the consultation among members will have a determinative value and will be either of a political or a juridical character, depending on whether the revision and the contents of the modified provision are determined by political or juridical factors.

However, the fact that Article XVII stipulates that requests for revision shall be addressed by the Parties to the North Atlantic Council, indicates that the Council is prepared to effect any kind of consultation between the Parties in order to ensure that the revision process is conducted to the satisfaction of all concerned.

The Council may intervene either by suggesting ways of conducting the revision process, which means that the Parties will have to consult each other in order to evaluate the Council's proposals, or by finding a solution, having first consulted the Parties on the advisability of the revision requested by them and, possibly, on the amendments to be made. In this case too, the consultations promoted by the Council may either be of a political or juridical character, depending on whether the request was accepted for political or juridical reasons and which prevailed in determining the amendments.

Article XXV of the Agreement on the Status of the North Atlantic Treaty Organization National Representatives and International Staff, signed in Ottawa on September 20, 1951, states that « the Council acting on behalf of the Organization may conclude with any member State or States supplementary agreements modifying the provisions of the present Agreement, so far as that State or those States are concerned », which, again, involves members of the North Atlantic Treaty Organization in consultation with each other.

This provision is a further demonstration of the important role the Council plays in the field of consultation between members ([5]). The Council is authorized to conclude with a member State or States, agreements which aim at modifying the provisions of the original Agreement signed in Ottawa. In order to do this, the Council must arrange consultations between the members to ascertain which supplementary agreement should be concluded and which provisions of the Ottawa Agreement should be modified. These consultations will either be of a political or juridical nature, depending on whether the modification of the agreement is founded on political or juridical considerations. For example, if the modification concerns a provision implying evaluation of a ju-

---

([5]) See Chapter III, para. 2.

ridical nature and the new rule is also founded on evaluations of the same kind, consultations will almost certainly
be of a juridical character; while they will be political
in cases where the modification concerns rules containing
an inadequate evaluation of a specific situation in which
the Organization, the representatives of member States,
the international staff or experts on missions for the
Organization may find themselves.

In this connection, mention should also be made of
Article XV of the Protocol on the Status of International
Military Headquarters set up pursuant to the North
Atlantic Treaty signed in Paris on August 28, 1952. This
Article provides for the differences between Parties or between any Party and any Allied Headquarters relating to
the interpretation or application of the Protocol to be
settled by negotiation between the Parties in dispute
without recourse to outside jurisdiction, with the exception
of cases in which there is an express provision to the
contrary. Differences which cannot be settled by direct
negotiation shall be referred to the North Atlantic Council.
This Article is very similar to Article XVI of the London
agreement quoted above: i.e. that the solution or settlement of the differences between parties requires in every
case a system either of political or of juridical consultation.

CHAPTER II

Organs Competent for Consultation

1. *General*

As has already been observed([1]), the main organ responsible for political and juridical consultation is the Council where, under the Chairmanship of the Secretary General, the Permanent Representatives of the member countries may raise any political problems which their Governments, or they themselves, consider merit discussion.

The Secretary General is another organ competent to handle consultation: he may initiate the discussion of questions and, by virtue of his chairmanship, has an important role in the deliberations of the Council.

2. *The Council its Function and Composition*

The Council was created on the basis of Article 9 of the North Atlantic Treaty, which provided for the establishment of this organ. Each of the contracting Parties is represented « to consider matters concerning

---

([1]) See Chapter I, para. 4.

the implementation of this Treaty ». In accordance with this Article, the Council « shall be so organized as to be able to meet promptly at any time » and « set up such subsidiary bodies as may be necessary ».

At its first session, in Washington on September 17, 1949, the Council indicated its principal tasks and these are essentially to assist the Parties in implementing the Treaty and particularly in attaining its basic objective. That objective is to assist, in accordance with the Charter of the U.N., in achieving the primary purpose of the United Nations: the maintenance of international peace and security [2].

During the first session, the Council determined its tasks, defining itself as the principal body in the North Atlantic Treaty Organization and taking upon itself the responsibility of considering all matters concerning the implementation of the provisions of the Treaty. Any subsidiary bodies set up under Article 9 of the Treaty are subordinate to the Council.

The organization established under the North Atlantic Treaty has operated until now with as much flexibility as possible and has been subject to review from time to time. Even though the Treaty regulates in a certain way the attributions and the tasks of the Council and of the subsidiary bodies to a certain extent, the establishment of this machinery does not preclude the use of other means for consultation and cooperation between any or all of the Parties on matters relating to the Treaty.

The Council itself is normally composed of Foreign Ministers, but should the Foreign Ministers be unable to

---

(2) See NATO *Final Communiqués*, p. 39.

attend, their places are taken by plenipotentiary representatives designated by the Parties. To enable the Council to meet promptly at any time the diplomatic representatives of the Parties in Washington are empowered to act as representatives of their Governments whenever necessary.

The Council at ambassadorial level is known as the Council in Permanent Session. It also meets at ministerial level when every State is represented by its Foreign Minister, although Defence and Finance Ministers have also attended these meetings. On four occasions, in 1957, 1974, 1975 and 1978 has met at Heads of Government level, when Prime Ministers and the President of the United States were present. At whatever level the Council takes decisions, the decisions are all equally valid.

Normally the Council meets under the chairmanship of the Secretary General and is serviced by the Executive Secretariat. It is convened by the Chairman and meets in ordinary session annually and at such other times as may be deemed desirable by the majority of the Parties. However, extraordinary session under Articles 4 and 5 of the Treaty may be called at the request of any Party invoking one of these Articles ([3]).

The location of each session of the Council is determined by the Chairman after consultation with the members of the Council.

It should be observed that all sovereign countries have an equal right to express their view and that political consultation within the Council ranges over the whole field of foreign affairs and is not limited to NATO's

---

([3]) For the contents of Articles 4 and 5 see Chapter I, paras 2 and 3.

geographical area. The only topics excluded are those relating to purely internal affairs of member countries (⁴).

It is clear that, in the Council in Permanent Session, the Ambassadors of the Member States act on instructions from their Governments and the Council has the role of a sort of « diplomatic workshop ».

Almost all Council meetings begin with the same item « Political Subjects », under which Permanent Representatives are able to raise and discuss in a restricted forum topical matters of interest to the Alliance: it is a way of holding political consultations. No official records are kept of these discussions in order to permit free and uninhibited exchanges. Whenever necessary, Private Meetings are held with an even more restricted attendance to allow for complete informality and confidentiality.

The subjects which come up to the Council for discussion and decision cover all aspects of the Organization's activities and are based on documents prepared by the Council's subordinate Committees. These documents contain recommendations which are then adopted unchanged or modified by the Council itself to reconcile divergent views and arrive at unanimously agreed decisions.

The decisions are taken with the consent of all Representatives or Ministers: there is no voting or majority decision. Council decisions, when adopted, become binding and can only be reserved by the Council itself.

Each year the Foreign Minister of a Member State is elected President of the Council; the selection is made in English alphabetical order of countries.

---

(4) See Schaus, *Le Conseil de l'Atlantique Nord* etc., p. 380.

3. *Committees Able to Hold Consultation*

In order to facilitate the rapid and efficient conduct of its work, the North Atlantic Council has established, in accordance with Article 9, additional political bodies. However, the existing informal arrangement for consultation between Representatives of the Parties has been maintained.

In Washington, on September 17, 1949, the Council established a Defence Committee with the task of taking the requisite steps for unifying defence plans for the North Atlantic area. The Defence Committee is composed of one representative from each Party; these representatives are normally Defence Ministers or their representatives. It was agreed that this Committee would meet at least once a year.

The Defence Committeee then established a Military Committee composed of one military representative from each Party and the Military Committee in its turn created a sub-committee known as the « Standing Group ».

The Standing Group is composed of one representative from France, the United Kingdom and the United States. It coordinates and integrates the defence plans and makes appropriate recommendations thereon to the Military Committee ([5]).

Even though the Military Committee and the Standing Group have essentially military functions, they should be mentioned here becouse of the relationship they may have with other bodies of a less military character, for instance, they maintain close working relations with the

---

([5]) These bodies were created in Washington on September 17, 1949, see NATO *Final Communiqués*, p. 43. The Standing Group was established on July 8, 1966.

Defence, Financial and Economic Committee, established by the Council in Washington on November 18, 1949.

This last Committee also has, in a certain way, military aims, being responsible for advising the Council on the financial and economic aspects of measures for the defence of the North Atlantic area. But, it can be considered responsible for consultations as it is also competent « to recommend financial arrangements for executing military defence plans and particularly financial arrangements for the interchange among North Atlantic Treaty countries of military equipment...; to measure and to recommend steps to meet the foreign exchange costs of imports of materials and equipment from non-member countries...; to consider, as may be found desirable and appropriate, plans for the mobilisation of economic and financial resources in times of emergency... » (6). All these arrangements require consultation, which can also, though not necessarily, be of a political character, among member and non-member countries.

Political consultation however, only started as a systematic exercise in NATO with the establishment of Council Deputies. This body was created at the London meeting on 15-18 May, 1950, in order to permit the Council to discharge fully its role as the principal and directing body of the North Atlantic Treaty.

With a Resolution of the same date, the Council, after having noticed that its meetings had « been too infrequent to permit a sufficient exchange of views on matters of common interest within the scope of the Treaty », established that each government should appoint a Deputy as its Council representative and that each

---

(6) See NATO *Final Communiqués,* pp. 49-50.

Deputy should be in the Council would be carried out effectively ([7]).

In the intervals between meetings of Ministers, the Deputies, duly authorised by their respective governments, will be responsible, on behalf of and in the name of the Council, for carrying out its policies and for formulating issues requiring decisions by the member governments.

In order to fulfil its duties, the Council Deputies must exchange views on political matters of common interest within the scope of the Treaty and promote and coordinate public information in furtherance of the objectives of the Treaty.

The Council Deputies established its headquarters in London and selected a permanent Chairman from among its members. The Chairman was responsible for directing the organization and its work. The Council Deputies was dissolved when the Permanent Council took over its tasks ([8]).

In the light of the recommendations adopted in April 1952, the Council started meeting in Permanent Session and extended the field of political consultation at the Lisbon Conference. At this Conference emphasis was laid on the importance of economic cooperation, the expansion and liberalization of trade and the possibility of working out closer cooperative arrangements with other bodies, particularly the OECD.

---

[7] See NATO *Final Communiqués*, p. 56.

[8] At the Lisbon Conference the Council drastically reorganized the Alliance's civilian agencies, starting with itself. The Permanent Council was to take over the tasks of the Council Deputies, Defence Production Board and Financial and Economic Board. See NATO *Final Communiqués*, p. 68.

The Council's powers were further increased by a resolution approved in April 1954, following which member countries were urged to submit to the Council all political information likely to be of interest to other members. It was during this period that the Council discussed Germany's situation and took part in the negotiation of the Paris and London Agreements, approved in October 1954 and the preparatory work for the Geneva Summit Conference during the summer of 1955 [9].

At the Ottawa meeting, held from September 15 to 20, 1951, the Council established a Temporary Council Committee (TCC) with the task of reconciling the requirements of collective security with the political and economic capabilities of the member countries. This body had to seek information, assistance and advice from all member governments, as well as from the military and civilian agencies of NATO, in order to establish whether the request of the military authorities could be accepted by the governments.

The Temporary Council Committee started work immediately after the Ottawa meeting. As it consisted of representatives of the twelve member countries, it delegated a part of its tasks to a three-man Executive Board composed of Mr. Averell Harriman (United States), Mr. Jean Monnet (France) and Sir Edwin Plowden (United Kingdom). With the help of this Executive Board, the TCC submitted a report to the Council on December 18, 1951, in which the political and economic capabilities of the member countries were reviewed. This report constituted the basis for the procedures subsequently adopted for determining the contributions individual member

---

[9] See Chapter IV.

countries could and should make to the common defence effort.

In 1956 the cold war was further accentuated as a result of the Hungarian insurrection and the situation in the Middle East, but the Council affirmed that the collective defence efforts of the Atlantic Powers had not been in vain and had successfully deterred Soviet aggression in Europe and had contributed to the adoption by the Soviet Government of the policy of coexistence [10].

It was at the Session held in Paris from May 4 to 5, 1956, that the Council, after having mentioned once again the principles of the United Nations Charter as the most apt for regulating the relations between the peoples of the Atlantic Community and « eventually also... the relation between the Soviet Union and the Western Powers » [11], decided to pursue peaceful initiatives « with the same energy that they displayed in building up their defence organization ».

In order to assist the Council in performing its tasks, the Council at Ministerial level, agreed to the formation of a committee of three Ministers to advise it on ways and means to improve and extend NATO cooperation in non-military fields and to develop greater unity with the Atlantic Community. This Committee on Non-Military Co-operation, more frequently referred to as the « Committee of Three » or the « Three Wise Men », was composed of Mr. Gaetano Martino (Italy), Mr. Halvard Lange (Norway) and Mr. Lester B. Pearson (Canada).

The report of this Committee was approved by the Council on December 13, 1956 and, both because of the

---

[10] See Chapter IV regarding cases mentioned in the text of this Chapter.

[11] See NATO *Final Communiqués*, p. 98.

moment at which it was presented (shortly after the Suez crisis) and because of its content, it represents the most important step in the development of political consultation, which increased as a consequence (^{12}).

In order to fulfil the multiplicity of its tasks, the Council, in accordance with a recommendation by the Committee of Three, established, in 1957, a « Committee of Political Advisers », later named the Political Committee.

This Committee, chaired by the Assistant Secretary General for Political Affairs, meets twice a week either at the level of Deputy Permanent Representatives or at that of Political Counsellors of Delegations. It prepares studies of political problems for discussion by the Council and submits reports to the Council on subjects to be debated. Moreover, it has the task of following up and implementing Council decisions. Besides this Committee, Ad Hoc Political Working Groups are engaged in political consultation relating to specific themes.

Groups of national experts, forming Regional Experts Committees, prepare studies on specific world regions for the Foreign Ministers' bi-annual discussion of the international situation.

The creation of the Atlantic Policy Advisory Group (APAG) which is subordinate to the Council represents another development in the field of consultation. The task of this Group, composed of senior Foreign Office officials from NATO countries, is to discuss long-term political problems without committing governments. Through its Chairman, the Assistant Secretary General for Political Affairs, the Group reports direct to the Council.

(^{12}) For the contents of this Report, see Chapter III.

On the strength of a proposal by the Belgian Government (specifically by Foreign Minister Harmel) and recalling an initiative taken by Canada in December 1964, the Council resolved, at the meeting held from December 15-16, 1966, to undertake a broad analysis of international developments since the signing of the North Atlantic Treaty in 1949. Its purpose would be to determine the influence of such developments on the Alliance and to identify the tasks which lie before it, « in order to strengthen the Alliance as a factor for a durable peace ». At the same Session the Council passed a resolution in which it was decided to carry out a study on the future tasks of the Alliance at a high political level. The studies were undertaken by Mr. Schültz, Mr. Watson, Mr. Spaak, Mr. Kohler and Mr. Patijn.

The Report on the Future Tasks of the Alliance, known as the « Harmel Report » was approved by the Council at the meeting held from December 13 to 14, 1967. This Report is in the tradition of the 1956 « Report by the Committee of Three », even though it is shorter (¹³). Its importance in the field of consultation consists not only in the fact that it indicates as necessary che participation of the USSR and the USA, in order to achieve a settlement of the political problems in Europe, but also and especially, in its description of the method to be adopted, namely a common approach to problems through greater consultation.

Apart from the organs or bodies indicated so far as the most appropriate for dealing with the consultation system, including those specifically appointed for it, there are also other committees set up by the Council which may carry out political consultations. For instance the

---

(¹³) See Chapter III.

Economic Committee, the Security Committee, the Science Committee, etc., all have to consult the governments of member countries in order to accomplish the work for which they were created, even though these consultations may not always be of an official nature. Many times decisions regarding the economy, international security, or scientific research are based on political factors and represent the outcome of much compromise and conciliation, made possible by the relationships developed between member and non-member countries as a result of the consultation system.

4. *The Secretary General's Activities in the Field of consultation*

From the above observations, it is evident that the Secretary General plays an important role in the field of political consultation. As Chairman of the Council he takes part in the most important activities relating to political and juridical consultation, he may initiate the discussion of questions and can determine the deliberations of the Council.

Since 1958 it has been the Secretary General's duty to present an annual report on political questions [14] to the Council. He may also offer, at any time, to help the governments of member countries settle their disputes and, with their consent, can seek a solution by negotiation, enquiry, mediation, arbitration or juridical settlement.

The Secretary General holds a special position in the North Atlantic Treaty Organization, which is com-

---

[14] See SCHAUS, *Le Conseil de l'Atlantique Nord*, etc., pp. 346-347.

parable with that of the Secretary General of the United Nations ([15]). He is represented on the Political Committee by the Assistant Secretary General for Political Affairs, who is Chairman. Similarly, his presence may be felt in the Atlantic Policy Advisory Group (APAG), which reports direct to the Council through the Political Committee.

The Secretary General also sits on the Regional Experts Committees and ad hoc Political Working Groups, whose activities are carried out by members of the International Staff under the direction of the Secretary General.

The Political Division, directed by the Assistant Secretary General of Political Affairs, is particularly engaged in the field of consultation. This Division is organized in three separate Directorates: Political Affairs, Economic Affairs and Information, of which only the Political Affairs Directorate and the Economic Affairs Directorate are of interest in this context.

The Political Affairs Directorate prepares the political discussions of the Council and the Political Committee. It also prepares notes and reports on political subjects for the Secretary General and the Council and all the working papers and reports for political consultation on the basis of the information supplied by national Delegations. For this purpose the Directorate establishes political liaison with the Delegations of the member

---

([15]) The obligation to present a political report was laid on the Secretary General by the Report of the Committee of Three. In his Report the Secretary General has to indicate the problems and possible developments which might require future consultation, so that difficulties might be resolved and positive and constructive initiatives be taken. The Secretary General can also request the assistance of the Permanent Representatives in order to settle disputes between Members pacefully. See Chapter III.

countries and with other international governmental and non-governmental organizations.

The Economic Directorate carries out similar functions with regard to all economic questions having political or defence implications of concern to NATO: it also maintains contacts with international economic organizations. Although its main function is in the economic sector, this Directorate may also play an important role in the political field, to the extent to which economic questions are connected with political problems and are regulated as a function of these.

At the conclusion of these observations, it must be mentioned that political consultations are not necessarily effected formally in all cases by the bodies expressly mentioned here or by other NATO Committees, but may also take place informally, through the regular meetings of Ambassadors and diplomats. This is also true of consultation between member countries of the Alliance; but, as will be specified later ([16]), consultations can also take place between NATO's member countries and countries of a different geographical area, or of a different political alliance, for example consultations between NATO and Eastern European countries. In this last case consultations are not always arranged by alliance organizations, but may be handled by individual member countries, which have previously decided a common political line by means of prior consultation, or by other bodies, perhaps after informal preliminary consultation among members.

([16]) See Chapter IV.

CHAPTER III

Rules Created by the Alliance in order
to Improve Consultation

1. *General*

The Three Wise Men's Report, approved by the North Atlantic Council on December 13, 1956, and the Report on the Future Tasks of the Alliance, an annex to the Final Communiqué of the Ministerial Meeting of December 14, 1967 [1], must be included among the rules created by the Alliance to enhance the activities of the Organization in the field of consultation.

Even though these two Reports are very different from each other in their content and length and the political atmosphere at the time they were drawn up was far from the same, they are of great importance to the subject considered here [2].

---

[1] See Chapter II, para. 2.

[2] Both Reports deal with other subjects besides that of consultation, but they will be examined here exclusively with reference to the subject of consultation.

2. *Three Wise Men's Report*:

a) Procedure

As has been mentioned [3], the Committee of Three, consisting of Dr. Gaetano Martino (Italy), Mr. Halvard Lange (Norway) and Mr. Lester M. Pearson (Canada), was established by the North Atlantic Council in Ministerial Session on May 5, 1956, in order to « advise the Council on ways and means to improve and extend NATO cooperation in non-military fields and to develop greater unity within the Atlantic Community ».

This Committee held its first meeting from June 20 to 22, 1956, at NATO Headquarters in Paris. On that occasion it established the procedure to be followed, deciding to send a questionnaire to each NATO member government in order to obtain its views on certain specific problems relating to cooperation in the political, economic, cultural and information fields. The Committee was also given the task of considering problems concerning the organization and functions of NATO.

In addition, the Committee issued a « Memorandum » containing explanatory notes and guidance to assist countries in the preparation of their replies to the questionnaire. After examining and analysing the replies to the questionnaire, the Committee held consultations with each member country individually. The purpose of these consultations was to clarify, where necessary, the positions taken by governments in their replies and to have preliminary discussion with government representatives on certain views of the Committee.

---

[3] See Chapter II, para. 3.

In order to fulfil its tasks the Committee tested the consultation system itself with the aim of examining and redefining the objectives and needs of the Alliance and of making recommendations for strengthening its internal solidarity.

3.   *b)* Principal Aims

The consultation system, which the Committee had set up to enable it to accomplish its work, highlighted the difficulties to be encountered in establishing cooperative coexistence between East and West. The cold war between the United States and the USSR had created tension, not only between States from different political and geographical areas, but also between countries from the same bloc and area. There was tension between members of the North Atlantic Treaty Organisation as well as between members of the Soviet bloc, where, in 1956, destalinization started and the Hungarian People's rebellion took place.

These observations may explain why the Three Wise Men's Report contain so many attacks on Soviet policy and why it insists so vigorously on conformity with its aims and cooperation between members, especially in the political field. At the present time, i.e. twenty-two years later, political cooperation represents a sort of « leit motiv » for it. In accordance with these statements the Committee expressed its conviction that the Atlantic Community can only develop greater unity by working constantly to achieve common policies by full and timely consultation on issues of common concern. If the members ignore each other's interests or engage in political of economic conflict, an Alliance cannot be effective either for deterrence or defence.

As far as the deterrent role of NATO is concerned, the Committee remarked that it is based on solidarity and strength and can be discharged only if the political and economic relations between members are close and members cooperate with each other.

4.   c) Defence-Cooperation and Political Consultation

The Committee of Three, recalled that, in the years prior to its creation, i.e., at the begininning of the Alliance, defence cooperation was the first and the most urgent requirement. But over the years many facts have proved that the strengthening of political consultation and economic cooperation, the development of resources, progress in education and public understanding, can be as important, or even more important in protecting the security of a nation or an alliance, than the building of special weapons. NATO can also be a tool for cooperation and progress if member Governments work to a much greater extent than hitherto, with and through NATO, for other purposes besides those of collective military defence.

This task, which the Committee recognizes as its own, is in accordance with the obligation described by the Treaty, which shows the Alliance as an association of the free Atlantic peoples for the promotion of their greater unity and the protection and the advancement of interests which, as free democracies, they have in common.

It is in order to comply with this obligation that the Committee recommended the use of sincere and genuine consultation and cooperation on questions of common concern. Recourse to the consultation system can help to achieve the harmonization of member countries' policies in relation to other areas, taking into account the broader interests of the whole international community, especially in the direction indicated by the United Nations, i.e., the maintenance of international peace and security and the solution of the problems dividing the world.

In the Committee's opinion, the consultation system represents a guarantee of survival in the nuclear age, when a nation on its own and relying exclusively on national policy and power, would not be strong enough to make any progress or even survive; while cooperating with other countries, it can live in security and can take the political and moral initiative to enable all States to develop in freedom and to bring about a secure peace for all nations.

5.   *d*) Presuppositions for Consultation

While the whole Report put great stress on consultation, it is especially in Chapters II and III, dedicated to political cooperation and to economic cooperation, respectively, that the Committee specified the aims and the meaning of consultation.

However, before considering the aims and the meaning of consultation, it is necessary to mention some presuppositions without which no consultation can take place. First, as the Committee rightly remarks, the consultation system must be accepted by the member countries. If one of them does not, or several, or all of them do not consent to it, it is destined for partial or total failure: in this instance one could talk either of consultation between some of the member States or of a refusal of consultation, but there would be no consultation in the sense that is covered here.

State have a way of refusing consultation available to them. This relates to questions of domestic jurisdiction and prohibits interference by other members. If all States taking part in an organization applied this method, it would paralyze the organization. But, even if the consultation system is accepted by the member States and none of them entrenche themselves behind the domestic jurisdiction clause, political cooperation can still only be achieved if there is a basis of confidence and understanding.

6.   *e*) Aims and Meaning of Consultation

One of the most important principles stated by the Committee in the Report was that the strengthening of political cooperation did not imply the weakening of the ties of the members with other friendly countries or with other international associations, since adherence to the Alliance was not exclusive or restrictive, neither did it contrast with European associations.

In order to justify its opinion, the Committee recolled what an earlier NATO Committee on the North Atlantic Community in 1951 had stated in a resolution: « The achievement of a closer degree of coordination of the foreign policies of the members of the North Atlantic Treaty, through the development of the habit of consultation on matters of common concern, would greatly strengthen the solidarity of the North Atlantic Community and increase the individual and collective capacity of its members to save the peaceful purposes for which NATO was established... » (⁴).

In this connection, consultation does not aim at isolating the organization or the Member States from other countries or organizations, but it constitutes a means to an end - harmonizing policies among member countries. In this way, consultation should always seek to arrive at timely agreement on common lines of policy and action; it is the opinion of the Committee that the members of the Alliance must make every effort to achieve this, since one must consider « impossible unity in defence and disunity in foreign policy ». But, having specified the aims of consultation as indicated by the Committee, the meaning which the same Committee has given to consultation should be explained.

The Report states that consultation within an alliance is more than an exchange of information, it is more than letting the NATO Council know about national decisions that have already been taken, or trying to enlist support for those decisions: « it means the discussion of problems collectively, in the early stages of policy formation and before national positions become fixed. At best, this will result in collective decisions on matters of interest affecting the Alliance ».

On the basis of this definition, consultation acquires a determinative importance in setting up the foreign policies of the member countries of the Alliance. Member countries must try to follow the suggestions of the Committee without giving in to the temptation of emphasizing consultation in words and evading it in fact, or by having recourse to it in cases where it is not necessary, with the result of justifying practices which unnecessarily ignore the common interest.

(⁴) See para. 43 of the Report mentioned above.

7. *f*) Limitations

The Committee of Three does not hide the fact that political consultation may, in practice, encounter many difficulties and may be exposed to some limitations. One of these, as already mentioned, relates to questions of domestic jurisdiction to which consultation cannot be applied. Moreover, the Council's observation that the ultimate responsability for decision and action still rests on national governments is of great importance.

It should further be observed that situations of extreme emergency may sometimes arise in which action must be taken by one government before consultation with other governments is possible: in this case it would be impossible to blame the lack of consultation on the State concerned as its behaviour was determined by necessity. These exceptional situations do not exclude, of course, the responsability to consult with their partners on appropriate matters, which lies on all members and should constitute the rule of the Atlantic Community; this rule may be broken only when there are no other possibilities open to States.

Another limitation stressed by the Committee regards the difficulty of specifying in advance all the subjects and all the situations in which consultation is necessary. In fact, it may prove difficult to separate by area, or by subject the matters of NATO concern from those of purely national concern, or to define the requirements and purposes of consultation. The Committee stated that « these things have to work themselves out in practice. In this process, experience is a better guide than dogma ».

Even though these limitations exist, the Committee noted that the essential thing is that on all occasions and in all circumstances, member governments, before acting or even before pronouncing, should keep the interests and the requirements of the Alliance in mind. In fact, if they neglect this fundamental principle, it may mean that the resolutions, recommendations, or declarations, even if they have been issued by the Council or one of the Council's Committees, will not be of any great value.

8.   g) General Suggestions on Matters of Consultation

After defining the difficulties connected with consultation, the Committee set down a number of suggestions in this matter, some of them of a general nature and others relating to specific recommendations.

Many of the general suggestions are directed at giving power to some of the Organization's bodies, especially the Conucil and the Secretary General [5]. In the opinion of the Committee members should inform the Council of any development which significantly affects the Alliance, not as a mere formality, but as a preliminary to effective political consultation. The Committee suggested that both individual members and the Secretary General should have the right to raise any subject for discussion in the Council which is of common interest to NATO and not of a purely domestic character. On matters which significantly affect the Alliance or any of its members, a member government should not, without adequate advance consultation, adopt firm policies or make major political pronouncements unless circumstances make such prior consultation clearly impossible.

---

[5] See Chapter II, para. 2 and 4.

Another consequence of NATO partnership is that member countries, in developing their national policies, should take the interests and views of other governments into consideration, particularly those most directly concerned. Moreover, where a community of views or consensus has been reached in the Council, the member governments should take this into account in the formation of national policies, offering an explanation to the Council if failing to do so. A consensus should be given full weight in any national action or policy.

The Committee calls for much closer ties between members and the Organization than the Treaty itself does. On the basis of the Committee's general suggestions, no State may make a move in foreign policy without first considering its own position in the Alliance and then that of the other members of without consulting, with a few exceptions, the various bodies of the Organization.

9.   *h)* Specific Recommendations

Certain specific recommendations were designed to give power to bodies of the Organization. For example, the Committe recommended that the Foreign Ministers should make an appraisal, at each Spring meeting, of the political progress of the Alliance, indicating the lines along which it should advance, thus strengthening their role in the consultation process.

The Committee also recommended that the Secretary General, in order to prepare this discussion, should submit an annual report analysing the major political problems of the Alliance. The Report should also review the extent to which member governments had consulted and cooperated on such problems and indicate the problems and possible developments which might require further consultation. The Secretary General should be assisted by member governments which, through their Permanent Representatives, would give him the information needed to prepare the report.

The Committe noted that effective consultation also required careful planning and preparation of the agenda for meetings of the Council, both in Ministerial and Permanent Session. It was, therefore, necessary for the Council to have background information and draft resolutions, if any, from all governments as a basis for the discussions.

A specific recommendation was made by the Committee regarding the constitution of a Committee of Political Advisers, which would come under the Council and have the Secretary General as Chairman. But, it is with particular reference to the peaceful settlement of disputes between members that the position of the Secretary General has increased in importance.

The Committee, having recalled the obligations for NATO's members deriving from the Charter of the United Nations and having reaffirmed the obligation of all members to settle any disputes between themselves by peaceful means, recommended that all disputes, except those of a legal or economic nature, for which attempts a settlement might best be made initially in the appropriate specialized economic organisation, be submitted to a good offices procedure within the NATO framework.

With reference to the good offices procedure, the Secretary General has been given powers so that he may offer his help at any time to the Parties in a dispute. The Secretary General has also acquired, as a result of the

Report, the same right and duty as the members, to bring matters which, in his opinion may threaten the solidarity or effectiveness of the Alliance, to the attention of the Council.

10. *i)* Political Consultation within the Framework of Other Kinds of Cooperation

The Committee observed that political cooperation is not reconcilable with economic conflict, meaning that in the economic as well as in the political field there must be a genuine desire among the members to work together and a readiness to consult on questions of common concern based on the recognition of common interests. Moreover, some of the economic interests shared by the members of NATO may also influence the political field, since they can lead to better relations among peoples and, under conditions of competitive rivalry, can promote human welfare. In these circumstances it is possible to achieve one of the aims of the Treaty, as set out in Article 2, i.e., the strengthening of the free institutions of the members and of other States.

Political consultation in the economic field may lead to the solution of economic issues arising between NATO and other organizations, especially when these issues attempt to divide or weaken the Atlantic Alliance or prejudice its interests. Such political consultation can have a determinative value in the resolution of economic disputes which may have political or strategic repercussions damaging to the Alliance. In this connection, the Committee, after remarking that « nothing would be gained by merely having repeated in NATO the same arguments made in other and more technically qualified organizations », proposed that any member or the Secretary General could raise issues in NATO on which they felt that consideration elsewhere was not making adequate progress and that NATO consultation might facilitate solutions contributing to the objectives of the Atlantic Community.

11. *The Report on the Future Tasks of the Alliance*

In 1966, on the initiative of the Foreign Minister of Belgium, Mr. Harmel, the governments of the fifteen nations of the Alliance resolved to study the future tasks of the Alliance and the procedures for fulfilling these tasks in order to strengthen the Alliance as a factor for durable peaces. A year later, in 1967, the Report was prepared on the basis of many studies by eminent people, and presented to the Council. which approved it on December 14, 1967.

After an interval of more than ten years, the Report appears to be concerned solely with the events of that period: the Berlin crisis, relations between NATO's members and Eastern European countries, etc. In this connection it should be stressed that the tension between Eastern and Western Europe had at that time been relaxed by measures designed to further détente and, because of the change in East-West relations brought about by the end of the cold war, the Report emphasizes that « the ultimate political purpose of the Alliance is to achieve a just and lasting peaceful order in Europe accompanied by appropriate security guarantees ».

The Harmel Report should be assessed as the continuation and development of the Report of the Committee of Three, even though it was prepared in different circumstances, is shorter and not as detailed.

The Report of the Committee of Three contains a

programme for the future tasks of the Alliance, but although the Harmel Report is concerned with the future tasks, it concentrates on reviewing the progress made in fulfilling the tasks attributed to the Alliance by the Committee of Three, thus the programme for the future takes second place.

The two Reports could not possibly have been similar, because, apart from the political situation, which was very different in 1956 and 1967, the Alliance was very young when the Committee of Three prepared its Report, so it had to look to the future and indicate the most appropriate means for achieving the best results. On the other hand, by 1967, the Alliance had elaborated its practices, based on years of experience. Accordingly, the Harmel Report had to take this experience into account and was thus able to indicate those tasks which were effectively achievable in the future and those which should be given up.

As far as political consultation is concerned, the Report points out that « as sovereing states, the Allies are not obliged to subordinate their policies to collective decision ». But, as the Alliance represents an effective forum and clearing house for the exchange of information and views, each member can decide its policy in the light of the close knowledge of the problems and objectives of the others. To this end the Report stated that the practice of frank and timely consultations « needs to be deepened and improved ». With reference to relations with the Soviet Union and the countries of Eastern Europe, the Report stresses that the chances of success would clearly be greater if the allies remain on parallel courses, especially in matters of close concern to them all; only in this way will their actions be more effective.

At the time at which the Report was prepared, the development of contacts between the countries of Western and Eeastern Europe was mainly on a bilateral basis. But there were and are certain subjects which by their very nature require a multilateral solution. For instance, the problem of German reunification, one of the most important faced by the Alliance, is considered in the Report as susceptible to multilateral solution between Eastern and Western nations.

With regard to crises and conflicts arising outside the area of the North Atlantic Treaty, the Report points out that the Allied countries can contribute individually within the United Nations and other international organizations to the maintenance of international peace and security and to the solution of important international problems. As these crises and conflicts may impair the security of the Alliance, either directly or by affecting the global balance, the established practice of consulting on such problems without commitment and as the case may demand, must be considered very opportune and profitable.

Consultation is thus assessed by the Report as the best means for fruitful discussion of the complex questions existing between Eastern and Western countries and for the maintenance of the global balance and international peace.

12. *Declaration on Atlantic Relations*

The principles propounded both in the Report of the Committee of Three and in the Harmel Report were repeated in the Declaration on Atlantic Relations approved and published by the North Atlantic Council in Ottawa on June 19, 1974, and signed by Heads of NATO Governments in Brussels on June 26, 1974.

This important document was signed after the commencement of negotiations between the NATO countries and the Warsaw Pact countries on the question of Mutual and Balanced Force Reductions in Central Europe (MBFR) on October 30, 1973, and after the start of the Conference on Security and Co-operation in Europe in Helsinki (CSCE) on July 3, 1973 [6]. This Declaration, which marked the 25th Anniversary of the Alliance, has a particular importance which stems from the fact that was solemnly signed by the Heads of the allied Governments.

In order to consider and evaluate this document correctly, it must stressed that it fits in with the practice adopted by the North Atlantic Alliance of conducting major reviews and adapting its policies to fit the changing circumstances. The period in which this document was drawn up, saw the passage from confrontation in East-West relations to an era of negotiation and for this reason it was more than ever necessary to preserve the cohesion of the members of the Alliance on the basis of frequent consultation. The Allies were convinced that the fulfilment of their common aims and, especially the relaxation of tension in East-West relations depended on the improvement of the method of consultation.

This opinion stems expressly from the Declaration [7] in which it is affirmed that close consultation is essential in order to foster « the conditions necessary for defence

---

[6] See Chapter IV.

[7] For the text of the Declaration, see NATO *Facts and Figures*, p. 340 and the Annexes of this study and NATO *Final Communiqués*. p. 318; for the problems exposed in the text see especially Article 11 of the Declaration.

and favourable for détente » and it reaffirms the need
« to strengthen the practice of frank and timely consultation by all means which may be appropriate on matters
relating to their common interests as Members of the
Alliance ». With reference to this, it should be observed
that, while the Report of the Committee of Three indicated the method of consultation as one of the most opportune means for achieving the principal aims of the
Alliance, the Declaration on Atlantic Relations approved
about twenty years later confirms the value of consultation, whose practice is recommended for the achievement
of the most important future aims and for the progress
of the Alliance.

CHAPTER IV

The Practice of Consultation

1. *General*

Since the institution of the Alliance the member States have acknowledged that the consultation system is the best instrument for achieving effective cooperation in all fields among themselves and for establishing relations with States outside the Alliance, especially with the Eastern countries. This is the reason why the consultation system has been the subject of so many and such important acts on the part of the Alliance [1] and why it has improved over the years, particularly by means of the establishment of more qualified bodies and organs [2].

From the practical point of view, the consultation system has been applied more and more over the years and its increased use and improvement has constituted a sort of « leit motiv » also at the meetings of the North Atlantic Council. It is sufficient to quote the declaration of the North Atlantic Council at the meeting in Ottawa on May 22, 23 and 24, 1963: « The growing scope and complexity of the problem facing the Alliance make it imperative for the Council to ensure that its political consultations are as prompt and effective as they can

---

[1] See Chapter II of this study.
[2] See Chapter III of this study.

be made. Ministers noted the progress already achieved in this direction and expressed their determination to secure still further improvements » (³). Precisely the same idea has also been expressed at many other meetings (⁴).

The concrete results of consultation, from an objective point of view, have been highly satisfactory in all ways. So, for instance, it was possible on the basis of political consultation to save the very existence of the Alliance following several important international events in 1957-1958 - such as the political integration of the Saar with the federal Republic of Germany, the accession of the United States to be Baghdad Pact, the signature of the Rome treaties setting up Euratom and the European Common Market, the reopening of the Suez Canal, the condemnation by the UN General Assembly of the Soviet intervention in Hungary, etc.

Mr. Bulganin, who was Soviet Prime Minister at that time sent an avalanche of letters to the member Governments. These messages raised a number of issues such as the calling of a summit meeting, the suspension of nuclear tests, the renunciation of the use of nuclear weapons, the institution of a de-nuclearized zone in Europe, etc. The letters were intended to create dissension among the members with a view to persuading the countries of the Alliance to negotiate separately with the Soviet Union. The NATO partners, on the contrary, decided to discuss within the Council both the contents of the Soviet letters and the draft replies prepared by each

---

(³) See NATO *Final Communiqués*, p. 151.

(⁴) e.g., in Paris on May 9-11, 1955, see NATO *Final Communiqués*, p. 161, in London on May 11-12, 1965, see NATO *Final Communiqués*, p. 161.

of the governments (⁵); in this way they were able to achieve a remarkable degree of harmony.

In other cases the consultations between one of the members of the Alliance and the USSR have supported the policy of détente pursued by the Alliance in East-West relations: for example, intense diplomatic activity between the United States and the USSR resulted, in the signature in Geneva on June 20, 1963, of an agreement on a « hot line » between Washington and Moscow. It led to the signature by the United States, the United Kingdom and the USSR of another treaty on August 5, 1963, banning nuclear tests in the atmosphere, in space and under water. This Treaty was open to signature by all countries. In other cases, consultation has led to positive results at international conferences, such as the Conference on Security and Co-operation in Europe at Helsinki on August 1, 1975.

This Chapter is devoted to the summary examination of some practical cases of consultation, although it will not be exhaustive, both because of the great number of cases of consultation and because of the difficulty of seeing the reports in them, since in many cases no documents are available, or, if they do exist, it is impossible to read them as they are subject either to diplomatic or military secrecy and cannot be consulted.

It is therefore practically impossible to specify the cases in which the North Atlantic Council has acted on the basis of proposals made by the Secretary or of other bodies and the cases in which it has worked independently.

Since the purpose of this Chapter is to emphasize the mechanism of consultation, it will not pay strict

---

(⁵) See NATO *Facts and Figures*, p. 42.

attention to the chronological succession of events, but will collect together, from a logical points of view, the most important international facts concerning the Alliance and relating to which the consultation system has been implemented.

2. Consultation Concerning Events outside the Area of the Alliance.

There has been no question in any part of the world in the last thirty years or so, i.e. since the constitution of the North Atlantic Alliance, that has not been the subject of consultation among members of the Alliance. It was of no importance if these events were might be of direct interest to only one or a few member countries or might apply within the area covered by the Warsaw Pact or in the area of the so-called « uncommitted » countries of Asia and Africa.

Apart, of course, from the problem of the accession of Greece and Turkey to the Alliance (6), the following

---

(6) The accession of Greece and Turkey was the result of political consultation among Members. At the meeting in Ottawa on September 15-20, 1951, the Council, considering that the security of the North Atlantic area would be enhanced by the accession of Greece and Turkey to the North Atlantic Treaty, agreed to recommend to the Member Governments that, subject to the approval of national parliaments under their respective legislative procedures, an invitation should be addressed as soon as possible to the Kingdom of Greece and the Republic of Turkey to accede to the Treaty (see NATO *Final Communiqués*, 19 Sept. 1974, p. 63). After opportune consultation at the meeting in Rome on November 24-28, 1951, the two States, pending parliamentary approval of the decision regarding the invitation, were invited to attend the plenary meeting of the Council, as observers (*idem*, p. 66). The Protocol of the accession was signed in London on October 22, 1958.

may be mentioned among the most important events to take place in the world outside the Alliance area, which became the subject of consultation: the Korean war ([7]), the extension of hostilities in Laos ([8]), the war in Indochina ([9]), the Manila Pact, 1954, setting up SEATO (South East Asia Treaty Organization), the Bandung Conference, 1955, of the uncommitted countries of Asia and Africa and the Baghdad Pact, 1955, to which the United States acceded in 1957 ([10]); this Pact became CENTO (Central Treaty Organization) on August 5, 1959.

Also among the events which took place outside the Alliance area that constituted subjects for consultation may be mentioned the Suez crisis and the situation in the Middle East.

([7]) The Korean war was discussed by the Council at its meeting in New York from September 16-18, 1950.

([8]) See the Final Communiqué of the meeting of the Council in Paris from April 23-25, 1953, NATO *Final Communiqués*, p. 78.

([9]) The question of Indocina was the subject of a resolution approved by the Council on December 15-18, 1952, in which it was affirmed, on the basis of former consultations, that « the resistance to direct or indirect aggression in any part of the world is an essential contribution to the common security of the free world » and that « the campaign waged by the French Union forces in Indocina deserves continuing support from the NATO Governments ». See NATO *Final Communiqués*, pp. 74-75.

([10]) At its meeting from May 9-11, 1955, in Paris, the Council stated that it had received reports of various security pacts on Middle East and Far East areas, including the Manila Pact and the Turco-Iraqui Pact. It welcomed the measures taken to strengthen the defence of the Middle East and far East areas. At the same meeting it also received a report on the Bandung Conference. In this connection, it expressed the hope that there would be a cessation of hostilities in the Far East. See NATO *Final Communiqués*, p. 90.

The Suez crisis culminated on July 26, 1956, in the nationalization of the Canal by President Nasser, the Franco-British military intervention and the invasion of Sinai from Israel. On this occasion the Council, after having emphasized the importance of consultation in order to settle international disputes by peaceful means, affirmed « the urgent need for initiating and pressing to a conclusion negotiations through the good offices of the United Nations with a view to restoring the Canal to full and free operation » ([11]).

During the hostilities in the Middle East between Israel and the Arab countries and just after a ceasefire had taken place, after the Six Days' War, the Ministers held an exchange of views on the Middle East situation at the Luxembourg meeting on June 13-14, 1967. They expressed the determination of the member countries « to support all efforts to establish a lasting peace in this area and resolve the outstanding problems in a spirit of equity and in accordance with the legitimate interests of all concerned » ([12]).

When hostilities flared up again in that region on October 6, 1973 (ending on October 24) between Israel on one side and Syria and Egypt on the other, the Ministers of the member countries consulted each other on the Middle East situation in Brussels on December 10, and 11, 1973; they welcomed the establishment of a UN Emergency Force and reaffirmed the support of all their governments for the relevant resolutions of the United Nations

---

([11]) See the Communiqué of the North Atlantic Council on December 11-14, 1956, in NATO *Final Communiqués*, p. 102.

([12]) See NATO *Final Communiqués*, p. 188. The « six days war » started on June 5, 1967.

Security Council and expressed their overriding concern to see a just and lasting settlement in the Middle East ([13]).

When, in 1962, a dispute arose between the United States and the Soviet Union over Cuba, the member States of the Alliance implemented the consultation process, even though this dispute concerned a State outside the NATO area. At the meeting held in Paris from December 13, to 15, 1962, the Ministers of the member States emphasized « the recent attempt by the Soviet Union to tilt the balance of force against the West » and gave unwavering support to the United States ([14]).

It is correct to say that there was no part of the world outside the Atlantic area which did not constitute a subject of consultation. Mention should be made here of the fact that, at the meeting of the North Atlantic Council in Paris from December, 14 to 16, 1965, the Ministers, after having noted that the tension had diminished in some part of the world, but that conflicts continued in South East Asia, declared that they had been informed by the United States Secretary of State that the United States remained ready to enter without preconditions into negotiations to end the war.

At that meeting, the United Kingdom Secretary of State for Defence outlined the British policy regarding Rhodesia and expressed appreciation for the support received from allied governments, stressing the need for further concerted action by members of the Alliance.

Consultations continued not only on these problems, but also « on those to which several Ministers drew atten-

---

([13]) See NATO *Final Communiqués*, pp. 304-305.
([14]) See NATO *Final Communiqués*, p. 147.

tion, arising out of the policies pursued by the People's Republic of China » (15).

3. *Consultation on Problems in the Mediterranean Area.*

Among the many problems concerning the Mediterranean area are two of particular interest from the point of view of consultation: the discord in Cyprus and the political position of Malta.

As is already well known, Cyprus achieved its independence in 1960 by means of treaties concluded between Cyprus, Greece, Turkey and the United Kingdom (16). However the composition of its population formed by Greek and Turkish communities, led, especially from 1964 onwards, to serious disorders between the two commuties, which had the natural effect of straining relations between Greece and Turkey.

In the face of this disquieting situation, the North Atlantic Council, anxious to preserve friendship between these two Members of the Alliance, made every effort to this end. At the Hague meeting in May, 1964, the Ministers reaffirmed the full support of their governments for the action decided on by the United Nations with a view to restoring law and order and for the efforts of the mediator appointed by the United Nations to seek an agreed solution to the problem (17).

---

(15) See NATO *Final Communiqués*, p. 167. At the meeting in London in May 1965, the Ministers considered other areas of tension such as Malaysia, Vietnam, the Dominican Republic, etc. See NATO *Final Communiqués*, p. 162.

(16) On the international « status » of Cyprus, see SAULLE, *La costituzione cipriota e il diritto internazionale*, in the *Rivista di diritto internazionale*, 1977, p. 579.

(17) See NATO *Final Communiqués*, p. 157.

The discord in Cyprus was discussed at other meetings of the North Atlantic Council, at which the efforts of the United Nations Force to restore peace to the island were approved and the Council endorsed the Secretary General's plea for an early resumption of constructive discussion between Greece and Turkey [18]. The efforts of the Council concluded with the announcement by the Foreign Ministers of Greece and Turkey that « the Governments of Greece and Turkey, inspired by a sincere desire to facilitate a peaceful and agreed solution of the Cyprus problem and to improve their relations, have decided to proceed to contacts and exchanges of views on the Cyprus problem and on Greek-Turkish relations » [19].

Unfortunately, the « coup d'etat » of July 1974 which ousted President Makarios was followed by a Turkish decision to take military action on the island. After the failure of conciliatory attempts in Geneva, with the help of the United Kingdom, aimed at achieving a compromise between Greece and Turkey, the Ankara Government ordered its troops to occupy more territory on the island which led to a serious crisis in Greek-Turkish relations.

At the annual meeting of the North Atlantic Council in Brussels in December, 1974, the Ministers heard a report by the Secretary General which reaffirmed the necessity for intensive consultations in order to reconcile the two Member countries. The Secretary General was able to work to this end by virtue of the Watching Brief for Greek-Turkish relations, conferred on him at the May 1964 Ministerial Meeting in the Hague [20].

With regard to Malta, the presence of NATO establishments and forces on the island gave rise to a problem for

[18] See NATO *Final Communiqués*, pp. 162, 168, 173.
[19] See NATO *Final Communiqués*, p. 173.
[20] See NATO *Final Communiqués*, p. 329.

70

the Alliance when Malta achieved its independence on September, 21, 1964. In November 1965, the Council adopted a resolution confirming the agreement of the Government of Malta to the continued legal status of the installations. In August 1968 a Working Group was created, under the authority of the Council, in accordance with the Resolution of 1965, in order to proceed with consultations and discussions concerning relations with Malta. The Government of Malta appointed a diplomatic representative in Brussels to represent Maltese interests in relations with NATO.

In July 1971 a change in the internal policy of Malta was reflected in international relations: NATO was requested to withdraw NAVSOUTH from the island. Although not a Member of the Alliance, Malta had been host to a NATO military headquarters for many years and this situation had until then, been accepted by all Maltese Governments.

After consultation between all the parties concerned, NATO acceded to the Maltese request and on March 26, 1972, the United Kingdom and Malta signed a seven year agreement on the use of certain military facilities on the island. The preparation of these negotiations, in which the Secretary General played a significant role, was the subject of particularly frequent consultation within the Council [21].

4. *Consultation Concerning Countries in the Warsaw Pact Area.*

Several events also occurred in the Warsaw Pact area, which were the subject of consultation among the Member

---

[21] NATO *Facts and Figures,* p. 74.

States. When, in 1956, the Hungarian insurrection was crushed by Soviet troops, the North Atlantic Council, after opportune consultation, declared at its meeting in Paris in December 1956, that « the brutal suppression of the heroic Hungarian people stands in stark contrast with Soviet public profession ». It also declared that « the people of Eastern Europe have the right to choose their own governments freely, unaffected by external pressure and the use or threat of force and to decide for themselves the political and social order they prefer ». The efforts of the United Nations to induce the Soviets to withdraw their forces from Hungary and to right the wrongs done to the Hungarian people, were supported by the members of the North Atlantic Alliance, who manifested their condemnation of the action of the USSR both within the Alliance and through their representatives, at the UN Security Council.

In 1968, when Dubcek tried to lead Czechoslovakia towards a more democratic regime, the armed forces of the Soviet Union and four other Warsaw Pact countries (Poland, Hungary, East Germany and Bulgaria) invaded Czechoslovakia destroying the so-called Prague Spring. With that invasion the Soviet Union elaborated its doctrine of « limited sovereignty » authorising the right of intervention in the affairs of other states deemed to be within a so-called « Socialist Commonwealth », if this intervention is necessary in order to ensure the triumph of socialism in that Commonwealth, especially in those countries where socialism is endangered.

With reference to the situation in Czechoslovakia, the North Atlantic Council, at the meeting held in Brussels in November 1969, after reaffirming the inviolability of the principle that all nations are independent and that consequently any intervention by one state in the affairs of another is unlawful, noted that this principle had been deliberately violated by the Soviet leaders with the backing of four of their allies. After consultation, the members of the Alliance denounced the use of force which « jeopardizes peace and international order and strikes at the principle of the United Nations Charter ». With their statement that « agreements concluded under the pressure of occupying forces can provide no justification for challenging this basic concept » ([22]), they also implicitly observed that treaties concluded under the pressure of military occupation were null and void.

But, it was especially with reference to the Alliance's problems that consultation should have been particularly intensive and important. At the meeting in November 1969 Ministers also declared that the intervention of the Soviet Union was dangerous to European security and gave rise to grave uncertainty about the situation and « about the calculations and intentions of the USSR ». Consequently, the allied countries should be very vigilant with regard to the Soviet Union.

Notwithstanding this, the Ministers recalled that one of the essential aims of the Alliance in the « establishment of a just and lasting peace in Europe » and for this reason they proposed, « while remaining in close consultation », exploring with the Soviet Union and the other countries of Eastern Europe « which concrete issues best lend themselves to fruitful negotiation and an early resolution ». They therefore instructed the Council to draft a list of these issues and to study how a useful process of negotiation could best be initiated, drawing up a report for the next meeting of the Ministers. The Council

---

([22]) See NATO *Final Communiqués*, p. 212.

stressed that any negotiations should be prepared well in advance and that all governments whose participation would be necessary to achieve a political settlement in Europe should take part.

5. *The Consultations on the German Problem.*

The main problem to test the Alliance's consultation system, which it did on many occasions, was that of Germany.

It is well known that at one of its first meetings, the North Atlantic Council discussed the defence of the **NATO** area against aggression similar to that in Korea [23], stating that a Forward Strategy should have been adopted for Europe. From this point of view Germany could make a very useful contribution to the defence of Western Europe.

After consultation, the Council reached unanimous agreement regarding the part which Germany might assume in the common defence and invited the Governments of the three Occupying Powers to explore this matter with the German Federal Government. Germany's participation in the Alliance commenced in May 1955, when it acceded to the North Atlantic Treaty.

Between 1950 and 1955 many events occurred which are of importance to the subject considered here.

In May 1952 a Convention on Relations between the Three Powers and the Federal Republic of Germany was signed in Bonn.

---

[23] See the New York meeting in September 1950 in **NATO** *Final Communiqués*, pp. 59-60.

In January-February 1954, the Foreign Ministers of the Big Four met in Berlin to discuss the problem of German reunification, but the meetings ended with no result.

Following a meeting in London, in September 1954, of the Nine countries (Belgium, Canada, France, the Federal Republic of Germany, Italy, Luxembourg, the Netherlands, the United Kingdom and the United States) held in London in September 1954 to seek an alternative to the EDC ([24]), a Four Power Conference (France, the Federal Republic of Germany, the United Kingdom and the United States) was held in Paris in October, at which a Protocol was adopted, terminating the occupation regime in the Federal Republic. At the end of the Conference a series of agreements was signed terminating the occu-

---

([24]) When, in 1952, it was decided at the Paris Conference to create a European Defence Community, the North Atlantic Council, after opportune consultation among the States of the Alliance, approved the initiative proposing to all Members and the European Defence Community reciprocal security undertakings between the Members of the two organizations. (See the Final Communiqué of the Lisbon meeting in February 1952, in NATO *Final Communiqués*, pp. 68-69, and the Resolution on the EDC taken in December 1952, idem, p. 75).

The principal aim of the EDC would be to settle the question of German participation in Western defence. But this Community never came into being because in August 1954, the French National Assembly refused to ratify the Treaty establishing it.

Another question that constituted a subject for consultation was the Trieste problem. In this case the agreements concluded by the two interested parties, Italy and Yugoslavia, in October 1954, were made known to the other Members of the Alliance by the Foreign Minister of Italy on October 22, 1954, in Paris. In this case the consultation consisted in a statement presented by the Italian Minister, in which he set out the value of the agreements from the Atlantic and European points of view.

pation regime in the Federal Republic of Germany and recognizing the Federal Republic as a sovereign state; Italy and the Federal Republic acceded to the Brussels Treaty (²⁵) and the Western Union became the Western European Union (WEA), establishing close cooperation and consultation with NATO.

All these events had been prepared for by means of consultations among the member countries of the Alliance, especially the Governments of France, the United Kingdom and the United States. This system was particularly useful on that occasion since many events took place concerning the Soviet Union, such as Soviet recognition of the German Democratic Republic in May 1953, the end of the state of war between the USSR and Germany, etc.

Just a few days after the accession of the Federal Republic of Germany to NATO, the USSR denounced the Franco-Soviet and Anglo-Soviet Treaties, concluded the Warsaw Pact on May, 14, signed in December a treaty with the Pankow regime, granting it the perogatives of a State and admitting it to the Warsaw Pact in January 1956.

After the political integration of the Saar with the Federal Republic of Germany, in January 1957, the Governments of France, the Federal Republic of Germany, the United Kingdom and the United States, signed a declaration, in Berlin, in July, affirming the identity of their policies with regard to the reunification of Germany and European security.

In November 1958, Mr. Khrushchev declared that the USSR wished to terminate the agreement on the status of Berlin and this declaration was immediately confirmed

---

(²⁵) See the Introduction to this study.

by the Soviet Government, which also announced its intention to transfer to the Pankow Authorities, within six months, all the powers it exercised in East Berlin by virtue of the 1945 agreement, including the control of communications between Western Germany and Berlin.

The North Atlantic Council, at its meeting in Paris, in December 1958, having noted the paramount importance of consultation, issued a Declaration on Berlin in which it asserted that no State had the right to withdraw unilaterally from its international engagements and that the methods adopted by the Soviet Union destroyed the mutual confidence between nations, which was one of the foundations of peace. The Council fully associated itself with the views previously expressed on the subject by the Governments of the United States, the United Kingdom, France and the Federal Republic of Germany.

The Council also recalled the responsibilities which each Member State had assumed with regard to the security and welfare of Berlin and the maintenance of the position of the Three Powers in that City. The Member States of the Alliance could not approve a solution of the Berlin question, which jeopardized the right of the three Western Powers to remain in Berlin as long as their responsibilities required and did not ensure freedom of communication between that City and the free world [26].

These principles were repeated to the USSR by the Foreign Ministers of France, the United Kingdom and the United States at the Conference on the German Problem which opened in Geneva on May 11, 1959 and which continued until June 19, when it adjourned until July 13, and finally adjourned on August 5. Throughout this

---

[26] See NATO *Final Communiqués*, p.123.

period close cooperation in the political field was maintained in the NATO Council between the three Western Powers and the other Allies. In addition to routine consultations, there were reports to the Council by the French Foreign Minister, Mr. Couve de Murville, and of the British Foreign Minister, Mr. Selwyn Lloyd, who were participating in the Conference.

These negotiations demonstrated the contrast in the positions of the West and the USSR with regard to Germany. However, the talks between President Eisenhower and Mr. Krushchev opened the door to further negotiation, at the level of Heads of Government, at the Summit Conference [27].

After the breakdown of the Summit Conference in February 1961, the Soviet Union in a note to the Federal Republic of Germany, reverted to the Berlin question. In August, as a result of a great number of people escaping to the West from East Germany, the Pankow regime barricaded the Eastern sector of Berlin and, despite the protests of the three Allied Powers, commenced the building of the Berlin Wall.

At the meeting in Paris in December 1961, the North Atlantic Council, after consultations among the Member States, declared that the USSR had artificially provoked a crisis over Berlin, cutting the capital of Germany in two. In the spirit of the agreed policy of the Alliance, the Council recalled the Declaration on Berlin, of December 1958, and reaffirmed its determination to protect and defend the liberties of West Berlin [28].

---

[27] See NATO *Final Communiqués,* pp. 139-140.

[28] See para. 6 of this Chapter.

From 1962 to 1971 the German situation represented one of the most important subjects to which the Council dedicated its consultation activities, even intensifying them. As a result of these activities, the Council affirmed many times [29] that a just and peaceful solution to the problem of Germany could be reached only on the basis of the right of self-determination, proposing in this connection, the reunification of the German people in freedom.

In May 1965, at the London meeting, the government of France, the United Kingdom and the United States, together with the Government of the Federal Republic of Germany, informed the Council of the solution to the German problem upon which they had agreed.

The Three Powers, known as the Group of Bonn [30], decided that the Council should make a declaration containing a proposal for the solution of the Berlin problem and suggesting means for close and continuous consultation between member countries of the Alliance. The declaration was made by the Council in December 1958, and demonstrated the value of consultation between the members of the Alliance and the Three Powers. Consultation continued throughout the following years and in April 1969 [31], the Ministers were informed, through the consultation system, that obstacles had been placed on freedom of access to Berlin and they supported the

---

[29] See the Communiqué of the Hague Session in May 1964, in NATO *Final Communiqués*, p. 156, the Communiqué of the Paris Session in December 1964, idem, p. 158 and the Declaration on Germany expressed by the governments of France, the Federal Republic of Germany, the United Kingdom and the United States, at the meeting of the North Atlantic Council held in Paris from 15 to 16 December 1966, idem, p. 182.

[30] See, SCHAUSS, p. 383.

[31] NATO *Final Communiqués*, p. 220.

determination of the Three Powers to maintain free access to the City.

At the meeting in Brussels in December 1970, the North Atlantic Treaty noted with satisfaction the signing of a Non-Aggression Treaty between the Federal Republic of Germany and the USSR and the initialling of the treaty between the Federal Republic of Germany and the Polish People's Republic on November 18, 1970. The conclusion of these treaties was welcomed as a contribution towards the reduction of tensions in Europe and as an important element of the « modus vivendi » which the Federal Republic of Germany wished to establish with its Eastern neighbours [32].

In September 1971, after years of preparation, many unsuccessful attempts and months of patient and intensive diplomacy, the Four Powers signed an agreement on Berlin, which would not come into effect until completed by the conclusion of the intra-German arrangements, reaffirmed the Four Powers' responsibility for Berlin and was designed to ensure unimpeded civilian access between the Western sectors and the areas under the authority of the German Democratic Republic.

The Ministers of the North Atlantic Council, in December, 1971 [33], declared that it should « bring about practical improvements »; and when the meetings between the Federal Republic of Germany (FRG) and the German Democratic Republic (GDR) started, they welcomed the progress made towards the conclusion of the agreements « as important steps in the effort to improve the situation in Germany ».

---

[32] NATO *Final Communiqués*, p. 244.
[33] NATO *Final Communiqués*, p. 267.

The Treaty between the two Germanies was signed on December 21, 1972, and was followed by a declaration by the Four Powers, in which they recorded their agreement and the fact that they could support the applications for membership of the United Nations when submitted by the FRG and the GDR, it being understood that these applications would be submitted simultaneously.

A few days before the signature of this Treaty, in December 1972, the Council ([34]) welcomed the initialling of the Treaty on the basis of relations between the FRG and the GDR and, in December 1973, after noting that the FRG and the GDR were admitted simultaneously as members of the United Nations in September 1973, the Council reaffirmed its view that the satisfactory development of relations between the German States could make « a significant contribution to the further relaxation of tensions in Europe » ([35]).

When, on October 7, 1973, the USSR and the GDR concluded a Treaty of Friendship, Co-operation and Mutual Assistance, the Council took note of a declaration made by the Governments of France, the United Kingdom and the United States on October 14, 1975, by which the rights and responsibilities of the Four Powers for Berlin and Germany as a whole remained unaffected by the Treaty between the USSR and the GDR. The Council, after consultation with the FRG, shared the view of the Government of that State, declaring that its policy of working for a state of peace in Europe in which the German nation would regain its unity through free self-determination, was « fully consistent with the Final Act of Helsinki » ([36]).

([34]) NATO *Final Communiqués*, p. 282.
([35]) NATO *Final Communiqués*, p. 305.
([36]) On the Helsinki Conference, see Para. 10 of this Chapter.

6. *The Summit Conferences and the Disarmament Conferences.*

The Summit Conference took place in July from 18 to 21, 1955, just after the accession of the Federal Republic of Germany to the North Atlantic Treaty and the signature, on May 15, 1955, of the Austrian State Treaty.

It was possible to hold this conference, because on June 7, the Governments of the United States, France and the United Kingdom sent a joint invitation to the USSR to attend a Four Power Conference. However, before the formal, joint invitation was sent, the North Atlantic Council had, at its meeting in May in Paris, been consulted by the three Western Powers about proposing negotiations to the Soviet Union in order to find a means of resolving outstanding issues; the Council welcomed this initiative [37]. The Soviet Government, on June 14, agreed to attend this meeting, which would decide a broad course of action, the details of which would subsequently be worked out at a longer conference of the four Foreign Ministers.

The Council declared that it hoped this initiative would lead progressively to agreements which would remove sources of conflict and contribute to the security and liberty of all peoples. In particular, it hoped that such negotiations might result in the unification of Germany in peace and promote progress towards the reduction, under effective safeguards, of armaments and armed forces. In that connection, it emphasized that the process of negotiation required « careful preparation »; and, with this intent, the Foreign Ministers of France, the United Kingdom and the United States consulted their

---

[37] See NATO *Final Communiqués*, p. 90.

colleagues at the meeting of the Council held in Paris on July 16, 1955.

During the Geneva meeting the consultations continued: the three Western Powers informed all the allied countries about the state of the negotiations and when the Summit Conference closed without any agreement, the Foreign Ministers of the Three Powers discussed, with their colleagues at the North Atlantic Council meeting on October 25, 1955, the plans and positions which they would present at the forthcoming negotiations at Geneva.

At this last meeting it was also declared that during the negotiations in Geneva, the governments of all the NATO countries not participating in the Conference would be kept informed through the North Atlantic Council and consulted further as the situation developed.

The second Geneva Conference was held at the level of Foreign Ministers and convened on October 27, 1955 closing on November 11, without any result.

The problem of German reunification was at the centre of the discussion and the position of the three Western Powers was in marked contrast to that of the Soviet Union. At the meeting in Paris in December 1955, the Council examined the international situation and approved the proposals presented by the three Western Ministers relating to: 1) the reunification of Germany through free elections, 2) the possibility for the unified German Government to choose freely its own foreign policy and, 3) the offering of a security pact to the USSR. With reference to the international situation and to East-West relations, the Council recognized, at that meeting, the necessity of « close co-operation between the Members of the Alliance, as envisaged in Article 2 of the Treaty » ([38]).

----

(38) See NATO *Final Communiqués*, p. 97.

Between 1955 and 1960 there was intensive diplomatic and consultative activity among member countries, in order to resolve the paramount problems of those years. Some of these problems concerned the defence of the Allied countries and disarmament. At the Bonn meeting of the North Atlantic Council in May 1957, the Ministers emphasized that there was a remedy for the fears professed by the Soviet Union with regard to the availability of nuclear weapons to NATO's defence forces. This remedy consisted of the acceptance of a general disarmament agreement embodying effective measures for control and inspection.

Since the United Nations Disarmament Sub-Committee was meeting at that time in London, with the participation of Canada, France, the United Kingdom and the United States, consultation between NATO's member States were closer and, thus, in accordance with the recommendations of the Committee of Three [39].

At the meeting in Paris in December 1957, which was preceded by the submission to the Disarmament Sub-Committee, in London in August, of the proposals approved by all the NATO countries and the talks in Washington, in October, between the President of the United States, Eisenhower and the Prime Minister of the United Kingdom, Macmillan, the member States, through their Heads of Government, re-examined their points of view, providing for: the reduction of all armaments and military forces; the cessation of the production of fissionable material for weapons; the reduction of existing stocks of nuclear weapons; the suspension of nuclear weapon tests; measures to guard against the risk of surprise attack.

---

[39] See Chapter III, para. 2 of this study.

At that meeting, the member States noted with regret that these proposals were rejected en bloc by the Soviet Union, although they had been approved by 56 members of the United Nations. They stated their willingness to promote, preferably within the framework of the United Nations, any negotiations with the USSR likely to lead to the implementation of the proposals mentioned above; declared that they were prepared to examine any proposals for general or partial disarmament and any proposal enabling agreement to be reached on the controlled reduction of armaments of all types. They also declared that, should the Soviet Government refuse to participate in the work of the next Disarmament Commission of the United Nations, they were prepared to call a meeting, at Foreign Minister level, to resolve the deadlock.

The possibility of a new Summit Conference was already being considered by the Member States in May 1959; in that connection the Council expressed the hope that it would be possible to resolve many important problems, such as the German problem, the determination of detailed measures for control over disarmament [40], etc.

The meetings of the Council in April and December 1959 were largely dedicated to the forthcoming negotiations between the East and the West: the negotiations on disarmament started again in Geneva in March 1960, within the framework of the Ten-Power Committee [41]. When the Ministerial Meeting of the Council took place

---

[40] See also the Geneva Conference, 1959, on the German problem, para. 5 of this chapter.

[41] The participants were: Bulgaria, Canada, Czechoslovakia, France, Italy, Poland, Rumania, the United Kingdom, the United States, the USSR.

in Istanbul, on May 2 - 3, 1960, the Summit Conference was very close and the Council continued with the preparations for this Conference. The Summit was opened in Paris on May 16, but an incident which had occurred a few days earlier contributed to its breakdown.

On May 1, an American U2 aircraft was shot down over Soviet territory and this event increased the incomprehension already existing between the Western Powers and the USSR. At the opening of the Summit Conference Mr. Khrushchev announced that he would go ahead with the meeting only on condition that the United States condemned the action of the United States Air Force and punished those directly responsible. President Eisenhower replied that the flights had been suspended and would not be resumed, but this did not satisfy Mr. Khrushchev, who broke up the meeting.

On May 19, the Foreign Ministers of France, the United Kingdom and the United States, reported to the Atlantic Council on the breakdown of the Summit talks.

Another consequence of this incident, a few weeks later, on June 27, was the abandonment of the Geneva Disarmament Conference by the Communist bloc countries, which asserted that the disarmament talks could only be usefully continued within a wider framework. Indeed, the Conference on Disarmament opened again in Geneva on March 14, 1962, with the participation of 17 nations, without achieving any results. It met again on June 21, 1963, and was adjourned until the end of July.

It was only in 1963 that relations between the United States and the Soviet Union improved with the signature in Geneva, on June 20, of an agreement for the installation of a « red telephone » between Washington and Moscow and with the signature of another agreement between these two States, on August 5, for the banning of nuclear tests in the atmosphere, in space and under water.

In January 1968, the United States and the Soviet Union agreed on the complete draft of the Nuclear Non-proliferation Treaty and tabled it at the Geneva Disarmament Conference: this Treaty came into force on March 5, 1970.

7. *Consultation as a Basis for Negotiation between East and West.*

In June 1966 the political leaders of the seven active members of the Warsaw Pact adopted, at a Summit meeting held in Budapest, the Declaration of Strengthening Peace and Security in Europe, in which they called « upon all European States to develop good neighbourly relations on the basis of the principles of independence and national sovereignty, equality, non-interference in internal affairs and mutual advantage founded on the principles of peaceful co-existence between States with different social systems ».

At a meeting in Reykjavik from June 24 to 25, 1968, the Foreign Ministers and representatives of the countries participating in the NATO Defence Programme adopted a declaration on « mutual and balanced force reductions » in which they proposed a series of measures in this field, including balanced and mutual force reductions, hoping that they could contribute significantly to the lessening of tension and to further reducing the danger of war.

In this connection the Ministers asserted the readiness of their Governments to explore with other interested States specific and practical steps in the arms control field; decided to make all necessary preparations for discussions on this subject with the Soviet Union and other countries of Eastern Europe and called on the latter to join in this search for progress towards peace.

However, the establishment of good relations between the Eastern and Western countries concerning the resolution of the main international problems was delayed by the occupation of Czechoslovakia (⁴²), in 1968.

In this climate, the declaration made by President Nixon in February 1969 on a visit to NATO Headquarters, which aimed at ending the period of confrontation with the USSR and at starting the period of negotiation, acquires particular importance. An answer to this declaration was embodied in an address by Warsaw Pact member countries to all European countries in Budapest in March 1969. This address was more moderate in tone than the previous ones and invited all countries of Europe to convene a General European Conference and to create the necessary pre-conditions so that this Conference would be successful and justify the hopes pinned upon it by the peoples (⁴³).

At the meeting in Washington in April 1969, the Ministers of the North Atlantic Council proposed, « while remaining in close consultation », exploring with the Soviet Union and other countries of Eastern Europe the concrete issues which best lent themselves to fruitful negotiation and an early resolution. In order to achieve this aim, they instructed the Council to draft a list of these issues and to study to see how a useful process

---

(⁴²) See para. 4 of this Chapter.

(⁴³) For the text of this address see *NATO and Security in the Seventies,* edited by Frans A. M. Alting von Geusau, Leyden 1971, pp. 135-137, and the annexes to this study.

of negotiation could best be initiated, and to draw up a report for the next meeting of Ministers. They decided, also, to prepare for the negotiations in advance and this clearly called for consultation between members [44].

The declaration of the consultative meeting of the Ministers of Foreign Affairs of the Warsaw Pact Member States in Prague, in October 1969, must be considered in the light of this intensive consultation activity in both groups of countries. Indeed, it was asserted that the participants in the consultations paid special attention to the preparations for the « all-European conference on the questions of security and cooperation in Europe », noting with satisfaction that the proposal to hold the European Conference had met with a positive response from most European States [45].

After opportune consultations, the Foreign Ministers of the NATO member countries, made a declaration at the Brussels meeting in December, 1969, regarding, among other subjects, the prospects for the negotiations. In this connection they asserted that the concrete issues concerning European security and cooperation mentioned in the previous Declaration of Foreign Ministers of the Warsaw Pact members, were subjects which lent themselves to discussion or negotiation with the Soviet Union and the other countries of Eastern Europe. The allied governments would therefore continue and intensify their contacts, discussions and negotiations through all appropriate channels, bilateral or multilateral, believing that progress was most likely to be made by choosing in each instance, the means most suitable for the subject.

---

[44] See NATO *Final Communiqués*, p. 219.
[45] See the text of this Declaration in *NATO and Security in the Seventies*, etc. p. 138.

The Ministers expressed their support for the bilateral initiative undertaken by some of the Members, such as the German Federal Government with the Soviet Union and other countries of Eastern Europe ([46]), with a view to reaching agreement on the renunciation of force and the threat of force. They declared that they remained receptive to signs of willingness on the part of the Soviet Union and other Eastern European countries to discuss measures to reduce tension and promote co-operation in Europe ([47]).

8. *Consultations on the Strategic Arms Limitation Talks (SALT)*

As a result of the intensive consultative activity among Eastern and Western countries and especially between NATO member States, the talks between the United States and the USSR on strategic arms limitation started in November 1969 in Helsinki and have continued ever since, either in Helsinki or in Vienna.

The first US-USSR conversations on this subject involved many sessions up to 1972. During this period the North Atlantic Allies were continuously consulted by the United States both in the North Atlantic Council and outside the organization. When the negotiations between the US and the USSR on this subject were near to the conclusion in concrete agreements (i.e. in the Treaty

---

([46]) These initiatives related to the signature of the German-Soviet Treaty in August 1970 and of the German-Polish Treaty in December 1970. See para. 7 of this Chapter.

([47]) At the Brussels meeting in December 1971, NATO *Final Communiqués*, p. 267.

on the Limitation of Anti-Ballistic Systems and in the interim agreement on strategic arms limitations signed in Moscow on May 26, 1972), the Ministers of the Member countries expressed their satisfaction with the close consultation maintained by the Alliance throughout the course of the Strategic Arms Limitation Talks and following the closure of the Talks, at the end of May 1972, they confirmed their satisfaction [48].

These agreements were preceded by the conclusion, the previous autumn, of agreements to reduce the risk of accidental nuclear war and to improve communication arrangements between the United States and the Soviet Union.

Negotiations between the two parties were resumed in Geneva on November 21, 1972, in order to study the development of a more detailed means of limiting offensive strategic weapons (SALT II). These negotiations had also been the subject of intensive consultation among the Member countries, which had been fully informed of developments and could express their own particular points of view. For example, at the Oslo meeting of the North Atlantic Council in May 1976, the Ministers of member States heard a report from the United States Secretary of State on the continuing United States efforts towards the further limitation of strategic offensive arms and towards the embodiment of the Vladivostock understanding [49] in a SALT Agreement. The Ministers discussed how the negotiations affected common security

---

[48] See the declaration presented at the Bonn meeting on May 30-31, 1972, NATO *Final Communiqués*, p. 276.

[49] At the Vladivostok meeting in November 1974, President Ford and Mr. Brezhnev reached an agreement on the limitation of US-USSR strategic nuclear arms.

interests and underlined the value of continuing consultations within the Alliance with respect to **SALT** [50]. Consultations on this subject are still continuing [51].

9. *Consultation on Mutual and Balanced Force Reductions (MBFR)*

The Harmel Report [52] indicated the possibility of making proposals for mutual and balanced force reductions. In order to comply with this suggestion, when the Ministers met at Reykjavik in June 1968, they adopted a « declaration » in which they expressed their belief that measures in the field of balanced and mutual force reductions could contribute significantly to the lessening of tension and to further reducing the danger of war. Having specifield the principles which could constitute the basis of negotiations, they affirmed the readiness of their Governments to explore, with other interested States, specific and practical steps in the arms control field [53].

At the meeting in Rome in May 1970, the Ministers representing the countries participating in **NATO's** Integrated Defence Programme recalled, in particular, the invitations they had addressed to the **Soviet Union** and the other countries of Eastern Europe to hold exploratory talks on mutual and balanced force reductions in Europe, with special reference to the Central Region [54]. At the

---

[50] NATO *Final Communiqués,* 1976, p. 12.

[51] See NATO *Final Communiqués,* 1977, p. 29.

[52] See Chapter III, para. 11.

[53] See NATO *Final Communiqués,* p. 209 and the annexes of this study.

[54] See NATO *Final Communiqués,* pp. 237-238.

Brussels meeting of the North Atlantic Council in December 1970, the Ministers noted that the Warsaw Pact countries had not given a direct answer to these invitations, but had mentioned the possibility of a discussion at some future date on the question of reducing foreign armed forces on the territory of European States [55]. The Ministers presented the Report on Alliance Defence for the Seventies at this meeting, after consultation among member States, in which they emphasized their hope of engaging the Soviet Union and its allies in useful talks on mutual and balanced force reductions and other disarmament measures.

The Ministers, at the Lisbon meeting in June 1971, noted with interest the response of the Soviet leaders which indicated their readiness to consider reductions in armaments and armed forces in Central Europe. They agreed that the Deputy Foreign Ministers or senior officials should meet in Brussels at an early date to review the results of exploratory contacts and to consult on substantive and procedural approaches to mutual and balanced force reductions. In order to improve consultation with the Soviet Union, the Ministers entrusted Mr. Brosio with the mission of exploring the Soviet opinion in Moscow.

Consultations between the member States of the Alliance and between Eastern and Western countries took place up to January 1973. The subjects of these consultations were the possibility of negotiations on mutual and balanced force reductions and related measures and the preparation of a Conference on Security and Cooperation in Europe [56]. The choice of these two topics for

[55] See NATO *Final Communiqués*, p. 24.
[56] See next paragraph.

consultation simultaneously demonstrated that, even if it were inappropriate to establish formal and specific links between these two problems, progress in one field of negotiation would have a favourable effect on the other.

In January 1973 multilateral exploratory talks on MBFR were inaugurated in Vienna, having been preceded by suitable exploratory talks; the formal negotiations opened in Vienna on October 30, 1973. Both before and during these negotiations close consultation was maintained, not only in the North Atlantic Council, but also in the Defence Planning Committee, demonstrating the importance the Alliance put on the problems of mutual and balanced force reductions. The Eurogroup also played a very important role in these negotiations. The Eurogroup created in 1970, was an informal group in the Alliance, gathering together member countries [57] and coordinating their defence efforts within the framework of NATO.

It is important to observe, with reference to the subject of this study, that in the case of the negotiations on Mutual and Balanced Force Reductions (MBFR), the Alliance assumed a managerial role. The Council in Pemanent Session, assisted by the Political Committee at senior level, decided the common positions of the allies and transmitted them as binding guidance to the ad hoc Group of Allied Negotiators in Vienna.

The principal objective of the negotiations was to establish an approximate parity between the two sides, in the form of a common ceiling for overall ground force manpower in the area in which the reductions

---

[57] The countries taking part in the Eurogroup are: Belgium, Denmark, the Federal Republic of Germany, Greece, Italy, Luxembourg, the Netherlands, Norway, Turkey and the United Kingdom.

would take place, taking into account combat capability. A first phase agreement was also proposed, providing for reductions in Soviet and United States ground forces in the area.

The final aims of the negotiations were to strive for an outcome which was both balanced and equitable and which would ensure undiminished security for all parties.

Although the question of MBFR is one of the main problems faced by NATO's member countries and has been the subject of continuous consultation ([58]), no agreement has yet been concluded.

10. *Consultations Regarding the Conference on Security and Co-operation in Europe (CSCE)*

As a result of an address, relating to the strengthening of peace and security in Europe ([59]), by Warsaw Pact member countries to all European countries in 1969 and the subsequent Declaration adopted at the Consultative Meeting of Foreign Ministers of the Warsaw Pact member States in 1969, this matter became the subject of close consultation between NATO members at the Rome meeting in May 1970. The Foreign Ministers declared that it would « not be enough to talk of European secu-

---

([58]) The Ministers pronounced on this subject at their meeting in Brussels in December 1973; in Ottawa in June 1974; in Brussels in December 1974; in Brussels in May 1975; in Brussels in December 1975; in Oslo in May 1976; in Brussels in December 1976; in London in May 1977; in Brussels in December 1977. See NATO *Final Communiqués*.

([59]) See para. 7 of this Chapter.

rity in the abstract ». At the same time they emphasized that the causes of insecurity in Europe were specific, being deeply rooted in conflicting ideas on State interests and observed that their elimination would require patient endeavour.

Member countries continued close consultation on this subject although they made the possibility of holding multilateral conversations on security and cooperation in Europe dependent upon the conclusion of negotiations on Berlin ([60]). Therefore, when relations between the Federal Republic of Germany and the USSR, the Polish People's Republic and the German Democratic Republic improved, they declared that they were prepared to enter into multilateral conversations concerning the preparations for a Conference on Security and Co-operation in Europe.

In order to achieve positive results on the subject of detailed and serious negotiations, the Member countries went into every aspect of the problem thoroughly and agreed on joint positions and aims for the preparatory conference in Helsinki in 1972-1973.

The progress of the preparatory talks in Helsinki provided ample proof that careful preparation by the allies and the coordination of the national positions of the member countries had been well worthwhile in terms of protecting allied interests and negotiating aims.

At their meeting in June 1973, the Ministers declared they were satisfied that it had been possible at Helsinki to agree on arrangements which would ensure that their proposals were examined fully and in depth. They stressed that constructive and specific results could be

---

([60]) See para. 5 of this Chapter.

achieved only through a process of detailed and serious negotiation without artificial time limits and then expressed their willingness to begin the first stage of the Conference.

The Conference opened in Helsinki on July 3, 1973, and on that occasion the NATO Member countries underlined the importance of the improvement in human contacts and in the free flow of information as an essential aspect of relations between States [61].

During the first stage of negotiations, which took place in Helsinki from July 3 to 7, 1973, the Ministers of other participating States adopted the programme of work submitted to them and issued instructions to the Committees and sub-Committees for the preparation, during the second main working stage, of definite proposals concerning the various items on the agenda [62]. The Ministers also set up a coordinating committee to harmonize the activities of the various conference committees [63]. The level of representation at which the CSCE would meet for the last stage was to be decided before the end of the second main working stage on the basis of the recommendations made by the co-ordinating committee.

The second phase of the CSCE took place in Geneva from September 18, 1973 to July 21, 1975. The third and final phase took place in Helsinki on July 31 and August 1, 1975, at the level of Heads of State and Government, who signed the Final Act of the Conference. In order to examine the implementation of the Final Act a Conference was called in Belgrade in 1977.

---

[61] See NATO *Final Communiqués*, pp. 294-295.

[62] See NATO *Final Communiqués*, p. 316.

[63] See *Testimonianze di un negoziato*, p. 446.

Both during the different phases and after the conclusion of the Final Act, NATO member countries continued consultation on the CSCE ([64]).

At the meeting in Washington on May 30 and 31, 1978, at the level of Heads of State and Government, the Member countries paid particular attention to the implementation of the Final Act in order to improve East-West relations. They observed that human rights nowdays constituted one of the main problems concerning the international community. They stressed the fact that the Belgrade Conference did not give concrete results, because some Eastern countries did not apply the Final Act to their citizens and they expressed the hope that the next meeting in Madrid, in 1980, would produce better results.

* * *

Two other cases should also be mentioned here. The first concerns the dispute, known as the « cod war », between Iceland on the one hand and the United Kingdom and the Federal Republic of Germany on the other, over North Sea fisheries; the second concerns the conflict between Greece and Turkey over the Aegean continental shelf.

11. *The « Cod War »*

The cod war ([65]) started on April 5, 1948, when the Government of Iceland passed a Law establishing a fish-

([64]) See NATO *Final Communiqués*, 1975, p. 26; idem 1976 pp. 11 and 27; idem 1977 pp. 13 and 27.

([65]) See RAYMOND GOY, *L'affaire des pecheries islandaises*, in *Clunet*, 1960, p. 370, R. B. BILDER, *The Anglo-Icelandic Fisheries Dispute*, in *Wisconsin Law Review*, 1973, p. 37; E.D. BROWN, *Iceland's*

ery zone within the limits of the continental shelf of Iceland.

Following the decision of the International Court of Justice on December 18, 1951, regarding the fisheries case between the United Kingdom and Norway (⁶⁶), Iceland passed a Regulation on March 19, 1952, providing for a four mile fishery limit and establishing the base-lines. The United Kingdom protested and the matter was discussed at the United Nations Assembly.

After the Geneva Conference on the Law of the Sea a Convention was signed on April 29, 1958, on the subject of the Continental Shelf, Article 2 of which established that coastal States have an « inherent right » to the area of the continental shelf and that extension of this area for the purpose of exploring the seabed and exploiting its natural resources constitutes the exercise of soverign rights.

On May 5, 1959, the Icelandic Parliament (the « Althing ») passed a Regulation extending Iceland's fishery limits to 12 miles and declaring that her right to the whole continental shelf would be sought. Both the United Kingdom and the Federal Republic of Germany protested.

There was an exchange of Notes on March 11, 1961, between the United Kingdom and Iceland, recognizing, with certain provisional clauses, the extension of the

---

fishery limits: the legal aspect, World To-Day, February 1973, p. 68; KATZ, Issues arising in the Icelandic fisheries case, in International and Comparative Law Quarterly, 1973, p. 83; R.R. CHURCHILL, The Fisheries Jurisdiction Case: the contribution of the International Court of Justice to the debate on coastal States fisheries right, in International and Comparative Law Quarterly, 1975, p. 82; RAYMOND GOY, Le Règlement de l'affaire des pecheries islandaises, in Revue Générale de droit international public, 1978, p. 434.

(⁶⁶) See I.C.J., Reports, 1951, pp. 116-206.

fishery limits to 12 miles and agreeing to take future disputes before the International Court of Justice. On July 19, 1961, there was an exchange of similar Notes between the Federal Republic of Germany and Iceland. In the exchange of Notes, both the United Kingdom and the Federal Republic of Germany recognized the fundamental importance of fisheries to the Icelandic economy and reserved their rights as « Third States » under international law.

As a result of the elections in 1971, the Government of Iceland declared its intention to extend the fishery limits and on February 15, 1972, announced that with effect from September 1, 1972, the limits would be extended to 50 miles from the baselines. The Governments of the United Kingdom and the Federal Republic of Germany protested.

In accordance with the exchange of Notes between the United Kingdom and Iceland and the Federal Republic of Germany and Iceland, the International Court of Justice, on August 17, 1972, issued its decision (with a dissenting opinion of judge Padilla Nervo of Mexico) in the form of two Orders, on interim measures for protection of the United Kingdom [67] and the Federal Republic of Germany [68].

On August 18, 1972, the International Court issued two Orders relating to its jurisdiction [69] and on February 2, 1973, it issued two separate but similar rulings (with the separate opinion of judge sir Gerald Fitzmaurice and the dissenting opinion of judge Padilla Nervo) establishing that it had jurisdiction to deal with both cases [70];

---

[67] See I.C.J., *Reports*, 1972, p. 12.
[68] See I.C.J., *Reports*, 1972, p. 30.
[69] See I.C.J., *Reports*, 1972, pp. 181 and 188.
[70] See I.C.J., *Reports*, 1973, pp. 3 and 49.

two Orders dated February 15, 1973, fixed the time limit for the written proceedings (⁷¹). On July 12, 1973, the Court issued two Orders relating to the continuation of the interim measures for protection, both with a declaration of judge Ignacio-Pinto and the dissenting opinion of judges Gros and Petrén (⁷²).

The most important event in the cod war was the extension by Iceland of her fisheries zone to 200 nautical miles, provided for by a Regulation dated July 15, 1974, and which entered into force on October 15, 1975.

On July 25, 1974, the International Court made two judgements (⁷³) concerning problems of jurisdiction and invited the parties in the dispute to reach settlement by means of negotiation. In an attempt to do this Iceland concluded separate but similar agreements on November

---

(⁷¹) See I.C.J., *Reports,* 1973, pp. 93 and 96.

(⁷²) See I.C.J., *Reports,* 1973, pp. 302 and 313.

(⁷³) See the Judgment of International Court of Justice of July, 25, 1974, *Fisheries Jurisdiction (United Kingdom v. Iceland), Merits, Judgement, I.C.J., Reports,* 1974, p. 3, with the declarations of Judges Lachs, Ignacio Pinto, Nagendra Singh. Judges Forster Bengzon, Jiménez de Aréchaga. Nagendra Singh and Ruda appended a joint separate opinion to the Judgment of the Court; Judges Dillard, De Castro and Sir Humphrey Waldock appended separate opinions to; Judges Gros, Petrén and Onyeama appended dissenting opinion to it.
See also the Judgment of July, 25, 1974, *Fisheries Jurisdiction (Federal Republic of Germany v. Iceland) Merits, Judgment, I.C.J. Reports,* 1974, p. 175.
This judgement is followed by the Declaration of Judges Lachs, Dillard, Ignacio-Pinto, Nagendra Singh.
Judges Forster, Bengon, Jiménez de Aréchaga, Nagendra Singh and Ruda appended a joint separate opinion to the Judgment of the Court; Judges De Castro and Sir Humphrey Waldock appended separate opinions to and Judges Gros, Petrén and Onyeama expressed dissenting opinions.

28, 1975, with the Federal Republic of Germany ([74]) and Belgium ([75]) concerning the extension of Iceland's fishery limits to 200 nautical miles.

No agreement could, however, be reached between Iceland and the United Kingdom and it looked as though the cod war might develop into a full scale war, especially when Iceland refused to negotiate in 1975 because the United Kingdom sent warships to protect her fishing fleet and Iceland closed her ports and airports to all British traffic ([76]). On a request from Iceland, the United Nations Security Council met on December 16, 1975, to consider the question.

The North Atlantic Council held an Extraordinary Meeting on January 12, 1976, at which Iceland declared her intention to re-examine her participation in the Alliance. The Council asked the Secretary General, Mr. Luns, to mediate, but negotiations failed and Iceland announced that she would break off diplomatic relations with the United Kingdom, if the United Kingdom did not withdraw her warships within 24 hours. The United Kingdom complied and negotiations continued in London from January 24 to 28, but without finding any solution.

The cod war reopened after certain events in February 1976 and the Secretary General was again asked to mediate. On February 19, 1976, Iceland broke off diplomatic relations with the United Kingdom.

Many attempts were made bilaterally to find a solution to the problem and the United Nations proposed that observers should be placed on the ships of the two

---

([74]) See *International Legal Materials*, 1976, p. 43.
([75]) See *International Legal Materials*, 1976, p. 1.
([76]) See GOY, *Le Règlement* etc., p. 530.

parties, but Iceland refused this proposal on February 24. The North Atlantic Council at its meeting in Oslo on May 20 and 21, 1976, discussed the fisheries dispute between Iceland and the United Kingdom [77] and as a result of the pressure exerted by NATO, the United Kingdom withdrew her warships on April 27. The negotiations concluded in Oslo with an exchange of Notes on June 1, 1976, allowing a maximum of 24 vessels per day, out of a total of 93 listed trawlers to fish specified areas [78].

12. *The Dispute between Greece and Turkey*

The dispute between Greece and Turkey concerning the continental shelf of the Aegean arose on November 1, 1973, when Turkey granted the Turkish State Petroleum Company (TPAO) exploration permits, which Greece claimed « encroached upon the continental shelf » around the Greek islands.

Turkey contended, however, that since the 1960's Greece had granted numerous exploration licenses and drilled for oil in the Aegean outside Greek territorial waters and declared, in 1974, that she was therefore entitled to start exploration within the limits of the na-

---

[77] NATO's position in the dispute — See ROUSSEAU, *Islande*, in *Revue générale de droit international public*, 1976, pp. 298, 611 et 944.

Oslo meeting — see NATO *Final Communiqués*, 1976, p. 14.

[78] Iceland also concluded an agreement with Norway on March 11, 1976; see GOY, *Le Règlement* etc. p. 534. For text of the Agreement see *Revue générale de droit international public* 1976, p. 993.

tural prolongation of the Anatolian peninsula ([79]). The boundary thus defined by Turkey included parts of the continental shelf around several of the Greek islands, i.e. Samothrace, Lemnos, Eustratos, Psara, Ikaria and Rhodes.

In an exchange of Notes (Greece sent the first Note to Turkey on January 27, 1975, and Turkey replied on February 6, 1976) the two governments decided to take the matter before the International Court of Justice.

As neither Greece nor Turkey availed themselves of the facultative clause (Clause No. 2) of Article 36 of the Statute of the International Court of Justice, which provides for compulsory jurisdiction by the Court, negotiations continued between the two countries from May 1975 until June 1976, before they reached a compromise agreement.

However, a series of incidents took place in the Aegean Sea between July 24 and August 15, 1976, which aggravated the situation and resulted in a series of Notes between the two countries protesting about each others conduct ([80]).

On August 10, 1976, Greece declared a state of « alerte avancée » and sent a request to the President of the United Nations Security Council for an urgent meeting of the Council on the grounds that recent and repeated

---

([79]) See ROUSSEAU, *Grèce et Turquie*, in *Revue générale de droit international public*, 1976, p. 1252; GROSS, *The Dispute between Greece and Turkey Concerning the Continental Shelf in the Aegean*, in the *American Journal of International Law*, 1977, p. 30.

See also the letter from the Permanent Representative of Turkey to the Secretary General of the United Nations dated August 18, 1976, UN Document S/12181.

([80]) See ROUSSEAU, quoted above, p. 1253-1254.

fragrant violations by Turkey of the sovereign rights of Greece over the continental shelf in the Aegean constituted a dangerous situation which threatened international peace and security ([81]).

Greece also instituted proceedings in the International Court of Justice against Turkey on the same day (August 10) and requested « interim » measures of protection. Security Council Resolution 395 (1976) afforded Greece a measure of satisfaction in some areas, but the Court failed to satisfy the Greek request for « interim » measures of protection ([82]).

NATO immediately consulted the two countries, asking them to use moderation and avoid risking a conflict through unilateral action ([83]). Consultation continued with the result that the Berne Agreement was concluded.

By an Order of September 11, 1976, the Court declared that application of Article 41 of its Statute regarding « interim » measures presupposes that « irreperable prejudice » could be caused to the rights of one of Parties of the dispute and that the seismic exploration carried out by Turkey were not, in the opinion of the Court, « creative of new rights » and would not « deprive the other State of any rights to which in law it may be entitled » ([84]). On the contrary, these explorations might be considered a subject for reparation by appropriate means.

([81]) UN Document S/12167.

([82]) GROSS, quoted above, p. 31-32.

([83]) See ROUSSEAU, quoted above, p. 1254.

([84]) See I.C.J. *Reports* 1976, p. 10, para. 25 and p. 11, para. 29; President Jimenez de Aréchaga, Vice President Nagendra Singh and Judges Lachs, Morozov, Ruda, Mosler, Elias and Tarazi appended separate opinions to the Court Order.

Turkey, on August 25, 1976, sent a communication to the Court in which it asserted « inter alia » that the Court had no jurisdiction to consider the Greek application. On October 14, 1976, the Court issued an Order fixing the time limits for the written proceedings on the question of jurisdiction, but without making any pronouncement on the matter ([85]).

Greece and Turkey signed an agreement on the procedure to be followed during the negotiations ([86]) on November 11, 1976. On April 18, 1977, the Court issued an order by which it extended the time limit to July 1977 for the submission of the Memorandum from the Government of Greece and to April 1978 for the submission of the Counter Memorandum from the Government of Turkey, postponing a decision on the subsequent procedure to be followed to a later date ([87]).

The North Atlantic Council maintained continuous consultation during the dispute, aiming at re-establishing good relations between the two countries. In fact the reduction of tension between these two member States had been the subject of consultation in the Council since 1964 ([88]) and was also the subject of a report by the Secretary General in connection with the Cyprus problem ([89]), upon whom the Council, at the Hague in May 1964, conferred a « watching brief ».

At the meeting held in Brussels from December 9-10, 1976, the Ministers of the North Atlantic Council voiced their satisfaction about the agreement between Greece

---

([85]) See I.C.J., *Reports* 1976, p. 42.

([86]) See ROUSSEAU, quoted above pp. 1255-1256.

([87]) See *I.C.J. Reports* 1977, pp. 3-4.

([88]) See NATO *Final Communiqués*, pp. 157 and 159.

([89]) See paragraph 3 of this Chapter.

and Turkey on the procedure to be followed for the delimitation of the continental shelf and expressed their hope that a satisfactory solution to this issue and the Aegean air space problem would be found [90].

13. *Other Recent Subjects of Consultation*

The North Atlantic Council held a meeting in Washington from May 30 to 31, 1978, at Heads of State and Government level, to consider some of the most important problems of the period.

Apart from the problems relating to Berlin and Germany, the implementation of the Final Act of the Helsinki Conference on Security and Cooperation in Europe, SALT and MBFR, all of which are usual topics of discussion, the meeting examined all question relating to international politics and all problems concerning the internal policy of States in a position to affect the international balance in any way.

There is no mention whatsoever in the North Atlantic Council's final communiqué of the last item, although several press agencies informed their readers that, for example, terrorism and Eurocommunism had been discussed at the Washington meeting [91]. Other items were,

---

[90] See NATO *Final Communiqués*, 1976, p. 30. At the meeting of the North Atlantic Council held in Washington from May 30 to 31, 1978, at Heads of State and Government level, the allies manifested their satisfaction about the talks between the Greek and Turkish Prime Ministers and their hope for a solution to the disputes between the two countries. See *Press Communiqués*, No. 36, June 12, 1978, para. 12 and the annexes of this study.

[91] See the Italian newspapers of May 28 and 29, 1978, referring to the information given by the press agency UPI.

however, specifically mentioned by the Council, such as the regional conflicts in the Third World and the USSR's role in them, as well as the need to settle such disputes by peaceful means.

The economic situation of some of the Allies was also considered on that occasion and the Heads of State and Government proposed the creation of a world economic system, which the Warsaw Pact countries were invited to join and under which the emergent countries would receive substantial aid.

The General Assembly of the UN, in Extraordinary Session from May 23 to July 1, 1978, discussed disarmament and passed a Resolution on June 30, 1978.

Even though disarmament is not one of the most typical of NATO's problems, as NATO was born and still is a military alliance, the Heads of State and Government showed their satisfaction with the results of the Extraordinary Session of the General Assembly, affirming the necessity to seize every opportunity to reduce armaments through negotiation and to use all means available to obtain stability and security in international relations.

CHAPTER V

Juridical Value of the Rules for Consultation
and of Consultation Itself

1. *General*

So far this study has shown that the North Atlantic Alliance has many rules for consultation [1] and that consultations conducted in accordance with these rules may differ greatly [2]. These differences may mean that the consultations have different juridical values which depend upon the rule and its source.

Some rules implicitly require consultation, while others explicitly call for consultation. The rules come from various sources, some being embodied in the North Atlantic Treaty or other international agreements concluded by the Alliance or its members, others being Recommendations or Declarations of the Alliance, adopted by its most important organ, the North Atlantic Council, and, thus, automatically adopted by the Alliance itself.

---

[1] See Chapters I and III.

[2] Examples of consultations are included particularly in Chapter IV.

2. The Juridical Value of the Rules for Consultation Embodied in Agreements

In order to explain the principal rules mentioned above from a juridical point of view and their connection with the differences in consultation, the doctrine of international law [3] should be recalled, according to which a preliminary agreement exists when two parties declare, by means of the exchange of acceptances, that they undertake: 1) to enter into negotiations concerning an agreement, 2) to conclude a future agreement, 3) to conclude an agreement in order to submit the settlement of a dispute to international jurisdiction [4]. The doctrine

---

[3] See LAUTERPACHT, *Private Law Sources and Analogies in International Law*, Oxford 1927, p. 159. CHAILLEY, *La nature juridique des traités internationaux selon le droit contemporain*, Paris 1932, p. 32; RIPERT, *Les regles du droit civil applicables aux rapports internationaux*, in *Recueil de l'Académie de droit international de La Haye*, 1933, II, p. 569; FITZMAURICE, *The Law and Procedure of International Court of Justice; Treaty Interpretation and Other Treaty Points*, in *British Yearbook of International Law*, 1951, p. 25; McNAIR, *The Law of Treaties*, Oxford 1961, p. 27; KELSEN, *Principles of International Law*, New York, 1966, p. 482; MIAJA DE LA MUELA, *Pacta de contrahendo en derecho internacional publico*, in *Revista espanola de derecho internacional*, 1968, p. 400; HAHN, *Das pactum de negotiando als völkerrechtliche Entscheidungsnorm*, in *Aussen Wirtschaftsdienst des Betriebs-Beraters*, October 1972, p. 484; FOIS, *L'accordo preliminare nel diritto internazionale*, Milan 1974.

[4] In addition to the doctrine quoted earlier, see also MORELLI, *La sentenza internazionale*, Padova 1931, pp. 15-16; SIMPSON-FOX, *International Arbitration, Law and Practice*, London 1959, p. 44. Some Authors also distinguish between the « pactum de contrahendo » and the « pactum de revidendo »; the latter being a treaty concluded in order to modify or to review a previous agreement. In this connection, see LECA, *Les techniques de révision des con-*

denoted a preliminary agreement of the first type a « pactum de negotiando », the second type a « pactum de contrahendo » and the third type a « pactum de compromittendo ». Moreover, the doctrine takes care to specify that there is no relation or connection between the concept of preliminary agreement in public international law and the general notion of preliminary agreement in the single state law systems (5).

If the definition of a preliminary agreement offered by the doctrine is compared with the rules for consultation in the North Atlantic Treaty, or in other treaties or conventions concluded by the Alliance or by its Members, it must be acknowledged that all these rules have character of preliminary agreements. Indeed, they result from an exchange of acceptances by the participants in every treaty or convention (6) with the aim of negotiating or concluding a future agreement or of submitting the settlement of a dispute to international jurisdiction.

Having established the above, it is then necessary to determine whether the rule in question should be considered a « pactum de negotiando », a « pactum de contrahendo » or a « pactum de compromittendo ». Thus,

---

ventions inetrnationales, Paris, 1961, p. 41. On the contrary the « pactum de revidendo » is included in the larger category of the « pactum de contrahendo ».

(5) Concerning the impossibility of applying the concepts developed by the doctrine in individual State systems of law to the international law system, see SAULLE, *L'errore negli atti giuridici internazionali,* Milan, 1964, p. 159; and *Appunti di Storia e di diritto dei trattati,* Roma, 1977.

(6) It must be observed that the doctrine regarding the preliminary agreement, quoted above, has treated this agreement almost exclusively as a bilateral agreement. It has not posed the problem regarding the possibility, admitted here, that it could also be a multilateral agreement.

for instance, Article 1 of the North Atlantic Treaty, according to which « the Parties undertake ... to settle any international dispute in which they may be involved by peaceful means » must be considered a « pactum de negotiando » because it contains the obligation to enter into negotiations in order to settle an international dispute by peaceful means.

Article 2, which states that the parties « will seek to eliminate conflict in their international economic policies and will encourage economic collaboration between any or all of them » must also be considered a « pactum de negotiando ». The elimination of conflict in international economic policies and the encouragement of economic collaboration involve an undertaking intended as an obligation, to enter into negotiations on economic matters.

Along the same lines, Article 4 contains the general obligation to consult. Still in the field of preliminary agreements, Article 5 of the Treaty lends itself to a different interpretation. The part of the Article which states that each Party, in the exercise of the right of individual or collective self-defence recognized by Article 51 of the Charter of the United Nations, will assist the Party or Parties attacked constitutes a « pactum de contrahendo », since it is an obligation to conclude an agreement and not merely to enter into negotiations[7].

Article 10 also contains a « pactum de contrahendo » in that it requires « unanimous agreement » in order to

---

[7] The problem posed in the text is similar to that considered by the doctrine with reference to Article 43 of the Charter of the United Nations. With reference to the interpretation of Article 43 of the Charter, see KELSEN, *Principles*, etc., already quoted, p. 482; FOIS, *L'accordo preliminare*, etc. quoted, p. 191.

invite any other European State to accede to the North Atlantic Treaty.

In order to avoid quoting all the rules contained in the Treaties concluded by the Alliance or by its Members, mention is made of Article XVI of the agreement between the Parties to the North Atlantic Treaty regarding the status of their forces, which was signed in London in 1951 ([8]). The rule embodied in this Article must be considered a « pactum de negotiando » where it relates to the settlement of disputes on the interpretation or application of the convention, but where it provides that the North Atlantic Council is competent to settle the disputes which cannot be settled by direct negotiation, it must be considered a « pactum de compromittendo ».

Article XXV of the Agreement on the Status of the North Atlantic Treaty Organization, National Representatives and International Staff, signed in Ottawa in 1951, must be interpreted differently. This Article states that « the Council acting on behalf of the Organization may conclude with any Member, State or States, supplementary agreements modifying the provisions of the present Agreement, so far as that State or those States are concerned » and it is clear from the way it is worded that it must be considered a « pactum de contrahendo ».

3. *The Juridical Value of Rules on Consultation Drawn up by the Alliance*

The rules, drawn up by the Alliance to improve consultation, especially those contained in the Report of

---

([8]) See Chapter I, para. 4.

the Committee of Three, in the Report on the Future Tasks of the Alliance and in the Declaration of Atlantic Relations (⁹) should be assessed differently. The principal problem connected with the juridical value of these rules lies in the lack of a provision in the North Atlantic Treaty, explaining the juridical value of the acts of the kind mentioned here that is to say lack of a provision like Article 14 of the Treaty instituting the European Coal and Steel Community. This last Article provides that the recommendations of the High Authority of the Community are obligatory for the members, even though they are free to choose the best means to pursue the aims indicated by those acts. For this reason the juridical value of the rules regarding consultation depends essentially on the obligatory character of the acts in which they are included.

As has been observed (¹⁰), there are many differences between the Report of the Committee of Three and the Harmel Report and these differences do not only relate to the length of these two reports or to the more detailed character of the first in comparison with the second. The most important difference between them concerns their different juridical values: while the Report of the Committee of Three may be considered a Recommendation (or a series of recommendations) adopted by the North Atlantic Council, the Harmel Report and the Declaration on Atlantic Relations may be considered international declarations.

In order to explain this opinion, it must be observed that international recommendations are acts of inter-

---

(⁹) See Chapter III, para. 12.
(¹⁰) See Chapter III, para. 11.

114

national organizations, usually with no obligatory effect for the members of the Organization: nevertheless, they may have such an effect when, as in the case of Article 14 of the Treaty of the European Coal and Steel Community, there is a provision which expressly confers that value on them, or, also, when they represent the basis of an agreement between the members of the Organization [11]. But, even if they are not obligatory, the recommendations always have a political and moral value, because the member States of an organisation have to pronounce in front of each other when they give their vote on the question which constitutes the subject of a recommendation [12].

A declaration is, on the contrary, an act of an international organization by which an organ asserts the value of certain principles, recognizes the existence of a particular situation, indicates to the organization, its members, or to other members of the international community, a programme or a task for the future [13].

If these observations are applied to the Report of the Committee of Three, there should be no doubt about qualifying this act as a Recommendation. Having defined consultation as « more than an exchange of information » and having asserted that it « will result in collective decisions on matters of common interest affecting the Alliance » (N. 42), the Committee (in Art. 51 of the Report) « recom-

[11] See SERENI, *Diritto internazionale,* II, Section II, Milan 1960, p. 1046.

[12] In the sense indicated in the text see, SERENI, *Diritto internazionale,* quoted above, p. 1053.

[13] In this way, SERENI, *Diritto internazionale,* p. 1053.

mended » many principles and practices in the field of political consultation, the most important of which is the following: « Where a consensus has been reached, it should be reflected in the formation of national policies. When for national reasons the consensus is not followed, the government concerned should offer an explanation to the Council. It is even more important that where an agreed and formal recommendation has emerged from the Council's discussions, governments should give full weight in any national actions or policies related to the subject of that recommendation ».

While there is no doubt that the Report of the Committee of Three should be classified as a Recommendation, there are many perplexities about the obligatory effect to be ascribed to it.

At the meeting in Paris in December 1956, the North Atlantic Council approved the recommendations contained in the Report of the Committee of Three and « invited » the Council in Permanent Session to implement, in the light of the comments made by governments, the principles and recommendations contained in this Report (14). It is clear that this invitation was not binding since both the Council in Permanent Session and the member governments which prepared the comments, were free to accept or refuse such an invitation. Accordingly the rules involving consultation contained in the Report have no compulsory value for the member States.

Another solution to this problem may also be offered — even if only hypothetically. As the importance of these rules has been reaffirmed on many occasions, both by the

---

(14) See NATO *Final Communiqués*, p. 104.

116

North Atlantic Council and by the member States, which always acted in accordance with these rules, it may be assumed that a tacit agreement based on the rules contained in the Report has been arrived at by the member States of the Alliance. If this interpretation, considered here as a mere hypothesis, should prove correct, it would follow that there was a binding agreement between members on the lines of the rules contained in the Report.

As far as the Harmel Report and the Declaration on Atlantic Relations are concerned, it is evident that they should both be classed as international Declaration, containing no obligations. In fact, they are acts in which the value of certain principles has been declared, the existence of particular situations recognized and a programme of certain tasks for the future indicated, which means that they are not binding for member States.

However, member States are obliged to consult each other in a large number of cases, examples of which are included in the hypothesis regarding the Report of the Committee of Three, the Harmel Report and the Declaration on Atlantic Relations. This may appear to contradict the foregoing observations but can easily be explained by the fact that the wording of the North Atlantic Treaty is very general and provides a wide range of possibilities with regard to consultation. The provisions are, in common with international agreements, rather abstract, but for this reason cover a considerable number of cases. Therefore, the rules drawn up by the Alliance to improve the consultation procedure have no value other than that of fulfilling, perfecting and detailing the general provisions contained in the North Atlantic Treaty, from which stems an obligation for member States to consult one another on matters indicated by the Treaty.

4. *The Juridical Nature of Consultation Provided for by the Various Rules*

The next problem to be resolved is the juridical nature of consultations. As has already been observed ([15]), this is strictly connected with the determination of the juridical nature of the rules, which usually resemble preliminary agreements, requiring consultation, either explicitly or implicitly. According to whether these agreements are considered a « pactum de negotiando » or a « pactum de compromittendo » or a « pactum de contrahendo », the juridical nature of the consultations will change depending on whether they concern a simple negotiation, the conclusion of an arbitration treaty (or a judical settlement agreement), or the conclusion of an agreement.

In order to explain this concept, it must be pointed out that when consultation is explicitly or implicitly provided for by a rule which can be defined as a « pactum de negotiando », it might represent only a moment but that moment may be the most important in negotiations which lead to the conclusion of an agreement. In just the same way, informal consultations may take place between all or some members of the Alliance in order to prepare for an important event or conference, in which case the consultations cannot end with an agreement.

A different assessment may be made of consultation when the rules can be defined as a « pactum de compromittendo ». In this case the consultations are included in the work leading up to the conclusion of an agreement where the jurisdiction is attributed to an international

---

([15]) See para. 1 of this Chapter. It must be mentioned that so far there is no bibliography on the subject of the juridical nature of consultations in general.

118

judge (or to an international body acting in the quality of an international judge) ([16]) in order to settle a dispute.

The consultations may not belong to the first phase of the negotiations, during which the negotiators usually exchange information and their views relating to the settlement of a particular dispute, or on the choice of the judge, but to the last and most important stage of the negotiations when an agreement is reached.

In this case it might be very difficult to establish whether there is a dividing line between consultation and the actual drawing up of the agreement. It may also be difficult to decide whether or not the consultations are an integral part of the conclusion and the actual drawing up of the agreement, as it is possible, and is, in fact, current practice, for every article of a compromise treaty to be decided by means of consultation between the contracting parties.

When there is a dividing line the consultations represent a separate stage consisting — as in the preceding case where consultation was provided for by rules defined as a «pactum de negotiando» — of an exchange of information or of a collective discussion of problems. When no division exists, the consultations, even in the case of a formal agreement, result in « collective decisions on matters of common interest affecting the Alliance » ([17]).

([16]) This is, for instance, the case of Article XVI of the London agrement, 1951, between the parties to the North Atlantic Treaty regarding the status of their forces. In this Article it is stated that the « differences which cannot be settled by direct negotiation shall be referred to the North Atlantic Council ». In this case the North Atlantic Council can also act as an international judge.

([17]) In this connection see the Report of the Committee of Three, N. 42 in NATO *Facts and Figures*, p. 316.

The foregoing also applies in cases where consultation is provided for by rules defined as a « pactum de contrahendo ».

5. *The Juridical Nature of Other Kinds of Consultation*

Apart from the cases considered hitherto, in which consultation is provided for by rules embodied in the North Atlantic Treaty or other agreements concluded by the Alliance or its members, there are many other types of consultation which are difficult to place in a certain category. This is partly due to the fact that member States decide to consult each other in instances not provided for by any of the abovementioned rules, or because the consultations are not conducted according to the rules, consultation being, perhaps, the only matter which, from a political point of view, can be left to the initiative of the members.

The reason for these divergences from practice to juridical provisions can be explained observing that, from a political point of view, perhaps no other subject as the consultations are fit for the free initiative of the States. On the other hand, the importance of consultation in the acts created by the Alliance and in its practice constitute a demonstration of the validity of these means in order to achieve the principal aims of the Atlantic Organization. Still from the political point of view it must be recalled that, during the years since the constitution of the Alliance, the technique of consultation has continuously improved, not only because of many acts providing for this improvement (such as the Report of the Committee of Three, etc.) have been issued, but also because of the refinement that has developed in consultations from their incessant use.

From the juridical point of view, recourse to some particular systems of consultation not being forbidden by the North Atlantic Treaty or by other international agreements among the Members of the Alliance, must be considered possible and permissible. Moreover, it may also be observed that the rules providing for consultations do not have the character of compulsory provisions. Therefore, the Member States could theoretically decide to derogate to them by means either of an express or tacit agreement on this matter. But, apart from this assumption, it must be pointed out that, in the absence of an appropriate and detailed regulation on this subject on the basis of an agreement, the Member States may interpret and apply the rules concerning consultation in a way that may be somewhat different from, although not in contrast with, the existing rules on this matter.

To quote only a few examples of these consultations, which may be considered as « atypical », it must be recalled that on many occasions the consultations are effected informally and may consist either in bilateral or in multilateral meetings. The atypical character of these consultations derives from the fact that either they are not provided for by the rules on the consultation mentioned above, or that they are provided for in a different way (for instance formally).

In order to determine whether these consultations complete their function at the negotiation stage [18], it should be decided whether or not they constitute an integral part of the agreement.

Examples of « atypical » consultation may be found in connection with the negotiations on Mutual and Balanced Force Reductions (MBFR) [19] and the Conference

---

[18] See para. 4 of this Chapter.
[19] See para. 9, Chapter IV.

on Security and Cooperation in Europe (CSCE) [20]. Consultations were held between the member States, either formally or informally, depending on whether they were connected with formal negotiations or confidential and unofficial meetings. Some of these meetings and negotiations were held within the North Atlantic Council or were promoted by the Council, others took place outside and were initiated by the members [21]. When the consultations, after the normal voting procedure, resulted in NATO member States taking a certain position at these Conferences, the consultations must be considered an integral part of the agreement.

The fact that some of the proposals upon which an agreement between NATO member States was based, had not received a majority vote at these Conferences and were, therefore, not approved, was of no importance. The consultations had succeeded in obtaining agreement among members, even though this was not destined to have any further consequences.

Apart from consultations of this type, many examples of which are considered in this study [23] (all of which

---

[20] See para. 10, Chapter IV.

[21] See FERRARIS L.V. (Editor), *Testimonianze di un negoziato*, Padova 1977, p. 13.

[22] See para. 4 of this Chapter.

[23] See especially Chapter IV. The consultations on the German problem, on facts which happened inside or outside the Alliance correspond to the hypothesis mentioned in the text. It may also be observed that, particularly in recent years, the practice of consultations has so increased that the Member States now consult on almost any subject: thus, for instance, terrorism and eurocommunism have also been the subject of consultation. See the international press relating to the meeting, at the level of Heads of State and Governments, in Washington on May 30 and 31, 1978 (See para. 13 of Chapter IV).

comply with the common practice of conferences) it should be pointed out that the consultations in connection with the Conferences on Mutual and Balanced Force Reductions and on Security and Cooperation in Europe were different even though they fall in the category of « atypical » consultation.

With reference to the negotiations on MBFR, the allied nations which were participating decided to negotiate on the basis of agreed NATO positions on all questions of policy and strategy. These common positions were developed in Brussels on the basis of national instructions by the Council in Permanent Session, assisted by the Political Committee at senior level. They were then forwarded as binding guidance to the ad hoc Group of Allied Negotiators in Vienna. Only in the case of day-to-day negotiating tactics was the guidance of the Council not required. As has been asserted (24), this was the first time in the history of the Alliance that a negotiation had been managed by the North Atlantic Council.

In order to qualify these consultations from the juridical point of view, it should be noted that the instructions, developed by the Council or by one of its bodies and given binding force, should be considered as obligatory recommendations, adopted by an organ (25), or, better, by a collegial organ of an international organization. With regard to this qualification, the hypothesis could be considered

---

(24) See NATO *Facts and Figures*, pp. 101-102.

(25) Some international recommendations may indeed have binding force, such as those of High Authority of the European Coal and Steel Community quoted in the text. This means that, on many occasions, there is no difference between a recommendation and a decision and that only the statute of an organization can indicate the different cases in which a recommendation instead of a decision has to be adopted. On this subject see SERENI, *Diritto internazionale*, etc., p. 1038; MALINTOPPI, *Le Raccomandazioni internazionali*, Milan, 1958.

— which in fact did happen — that one or more of the member States did not follow such binding instructions. It would be clear, under this hypothesis that the lack of observance, on the part of one or more member States, of these instructions developed by the Council or by its body, would be considered a violation of the obligations by that or those member States towards the Alliance and, therefore, as an illicit act in international law.

The consultations between the member States with regard to the Conference on Security and Cooperation in Europe (CSCE) were different from the MBFR consultation. Not only were major problems examined by the Council and other NATO Committees in Brussels, but, through negotiations, there was the closest possible day-to-day coordination of positions between the delegations of the Alliance countries at the Conference itself ([26]). However a distinction must be made between consultation effected within the Council and the day-to-day coordination between the delegations of the Alliance countries at the conference itself. Consultation might also end in the development of binding instructions having the same value as the instructions developed by the Council with regard to the MBFR Conference; the second may be assessed as an activity of negotiation among the member States of the Alliance, possibly involving an agreement or several agreements between them on the individual questions encountered during the Conference.

Before ending this study, it should be mentioned that consultation between member States of NATO and States belonging to other international organizations fall into the category of normal negotiations between States or organizations and are, therefore, not considered here.

([26]) See NATO *Facts and Figures*, p. 102.

GENERAL BIBLIOGRAPHY

Apart from the authors quoted in the study, see also:

ALTING VON GEUSAU, *NATO and Developments in Eastern Europe*, in *NATO and Security in the Seventies*, p. 59.

ALTING VON GEUSAU, *Planning Ahead; Security and Cooperation in the Seventies*, in *NATO and Security in the Seventies*, p. 103.

BECKETT, *The North Atlantic Treaty, the Brussels Treaty and the Charter of the United Nations*, London 1950.

BENTIVOGLIO, *Strutture Istituzionali ed Organizzative della NATO*, in *La NATO, Problemi e prospettive*, Milan 1967, p. 55.

BOWETT, *Self-Defence in international law*, Manchester, 1958.

CASSONI, *La posizione della NATO e dei Quartieri Generali nell'ambito dell'ordinamento italiano*, in *La NATO, Problemi e prospettive*, quoted, p. 69.

FENWICK, *The Atlantic Pact*, in *American Journal of International Law*, 1949, p. 312.

FERRI, C. E., *Modi e Strumenti d'Attuazione dell'articolo 2 del Patto Atlantico*, in *NATO, problemi e prospettive*, quoted, p. 99.

GOODHART, Arthur Lohman, *the North Atlantic Treaty of* 1949, in *Academie de droit international de La Haye*, Recueil des Cours, 1951, II, p. 183-236.

KELSEN, *Is the North Atlantic Treaty a regional arrangement?*, in *American Journal of International Law*, 1951, p. 162.

KISSINGER, *NATO: evolution or decline*, in *American Foreign Policy in International Perspective*, 1971, pp. 262-269.

VAN KLEFFENS, *Regionalisme and Political Pacts with Special Reference to the North Atlantic Treaty Organization*, in *American Journal of International Law*, 1949, p. 666.

127

MONACO, *Lezioni di organizzazione internazionale, II, Diritto dell'integrazione europea,* Turin 1975, II edition.

MOSCA, *Storia di un'Alleanza,* in *NATO, problemi e prospettive,* quoted, p. 29.

ROBERTSON, *European Institutions, Co-operation, integration, unification,* London 1966.

SERENI, *Le organizzazioni internazionali,* Milan 1959.

SIBERT, *OTAN, origines, mécanisme, nature,* in *Revue générale de droit international public,* 1956.

SILVESTRI, *NATO and the Mediterranean Situation,* in *NATO and Security in the Seventies.* Leyden, 1971, p. 43 ss.

BIBLIOGRAPHY ON LIMITATION OF FORCES

BARNETT, *Trans-SALT: Soviet Strategic Doctrine in Orbis* 1975.

BIDDLE, *Weapons Technology and Arms Control,* New York, 1972.

EPSTEIN, *Disarmament: Twenty-Five Years of Effort,* Toronto 1971.

FISCHER, *The Non-Proliferation of Nuclear Weapons,* New York 1972.

FORNDRAN, E., *Probleme der Internationalen Abrüstung,* Frankfurt au Mein 1970.

KOLKOWICZ, *The Soviet Union and Arms Control: A superpower Dilemma,* Baltimore 1970.

ROBERTS, *The Nuclear Years: the Arms Race and Arms Control 1945-70,* New York 1970.

YOUNG, *A Farewell to Arms Control?,* Baltimore 1972.

For the different aspects of the Alliance, COLIN GORDON, *The Atlantic Alliance, a bibliography,* London - New York 1978.

ANNEXES

THE NORTH ATLANTIC TREATY

Washington D.C., April 4, 1949

The Parties to this Treaty reaffirm their faith in the purposes and principles of the Charter of the United Nations and their desire to live in peace with all peoples and all governments.

They are determined to safeguard the freedom, common heritage and civilization of their peoples, founded on the principles of democracy, individual liberty and the rule of law.

They seek to promote stability and well-being in the North Atlantic area.

They are resolved to unite their efforts for collective defence and for the preservation of peace and security.

They therefore agree to this North Atlantic Treaty:

Article 1

The Parties undertake, as set forth in the Charter of the United Nations, to settle any international dispute in which they may be involved by peaceful means in such a manner that international peace and security and justice are not endangered, and to refrain in their international relations from the threat or use of force in any manner inconsistent with the purposes of the United Nations.

Article 2

The Parties will contribute toward the further development of peaceful and friendly international relations by strengthening their free institutions, by bringing about a better understanding of the principles upon which these institutions are founded, and by promoting conditions of stability and well-being. They will seek to eliminate conflict in their international economic policies and will encourage economic collaboration between any or all of them.

Article 3

In order more effectively to achieve the objectives of this Treaty, the Parties, separately and jointly, by means of continuous and effective self-help and mutual aid, will maintain and develop their individual and collective capacity to resist armed attack.

Article 4

The Parties will consult together whenever, in the opinion of any of them, the territorial integrity, political independence or security of any of the Parties is threatened.

Article 5

The Parties agree that an armed attack against one or more of them in Europe or North America shall be considered an attack against them all and consequently they agree that, if such an armed attack occurs, each of them, in exercise of the right of individual or collective self-defence recognized by Article 51 of the Charter of the United Nations, will assist the Party or Parties so attacked by taking forthwith, individually and in concert with the other Parties, such action as it deems necessary, including the use of armed force, to restore and maintain the security of the North Atlantic area.

Any such armed attack and all measures taken as a result thereof shall immediately be reported to the Security Council. Such measures shall be terminated when the Security Council has taken the measures necessary to restore and maintain international peace and security.

Article 6 ([1])

For the purpose of Article V an armed attack on one or more of the Parties is deemed to include an armed attack on the territory of any of the Parties in Europe or North America, on the Algerian Departments of France ([2]), on the occupation forces of any Party in Europe, on the islands under the jurisdiction of any Party in the North Atlantic area north of the Tropic of Cancer or on the vessels or aircraft in this area of any of the Parties.

([1]) The definition of the territories to which Article V applies has been revised by Article II of the Protocol to the North Atlantic Treaty on the accession of Greece and Turkey.

([2]) On January 16, 1963, the North Atlantic Council has heard a declaration by the French Representative who recalled that by the vote on self-determination on July 1, 1962, the Algerian people had pronounced itself in favour of the independence of Algeria in co-operation with France. In consequence, the President of the French Republic had on July 3, 1962, formally recognized the independence of Algeria. The result was that the « Algerian departments of France » no longer existed as such, and that at the same time the fact that they were mentioned in the North Atlantic Treaty had no longer any bearing.

Following this statement the Council noted that insofar as the former Algerian Departments of France were concerned, the relevant clauses of this Treaty had become inapplicable as from July 3, 1962.

Article 7

This Treaty does not affect, and shall not be interpreted as affecting, in any way the rights and obligations under the Charter of the Parties which are members of the United Nations, or the primary responsibility of the Security Council for the maintenance of international peace and security.

Article 8

Each Party declares that none of the international engagements now in force between it and any other of the Parties or any third State is in conflict with the provisions of this Treaty, and undertakes not to enter into any international engagement in conflict with this Treaty.

Article 9

The Parties hereby establish a Council, on which each of them shall be represented, to consider matters concerning the implementation of this Treaty. The Council shall be so organized as to be able to meet promptly at any time. The Council shall set up such subsidiary bodies as may be necessary; in particular it shall establish immediately a defence committee which shall recommend measures for the implementation of Articles III and V.

Article 10

The Parties may, by unanimous agreement, invite any other European State in a position to further the principles of this Treaty and to contribute to the security of the North Atlantic area to accede to this Treaty. Any

State so invited may become a Party to the Treaty by depositing its instrument of accession with the Government of the United States of America. The Government of the United States of America will inform each of the Parties of the deposit of each such instrument of accession.

Article 11

This Treaty shall be ratified and its provisions carried out by the Parties in accordance with their respective constitutional processes. The instruments of ratification shall be deposited as soon as possible with the Government of the United States of America, which will notify all the other signatories of each deposit. The Treaty shall enter into force between the States which have ratified it as soon as the ratifications of the majority of the signatories, including the ratifications of Belgium, Canada, France, Luxembourg, the Netherlands, the United Kingdom and the United States, have been deposited and shall come into effect with respect to other States on the date of the deposit of their ratifications.

Article 12

After the Treaty has been in force for ten years, or at any time thereafter, the Parties shall, if any of them so requests, consult together for the purpose of reviewing the Treaty, having regard for the factors then affecting peace and security in the North Atlantic area, including the development of universal as well as regional arrangements under the Charter of the United Nations for the maintenance of international peace and security.

Article 13

After the Treaty has been in force for twenty years, any Party may cease to be a Party one year after its notice of denunciation has been given to the Government of the United States of America, which will inform the Governments of the other Parties of the deposit of each notice of denunciation.

Article 14

This Treaty, of which the English and French texts are equally authentic, shall be deposited in the archives of the Government of the United States of America. Duly certified copies will be transmitted by that Government to the Governments of other signatories.

THE WARSAW PACT DECLARATION

At a summit meeting held in Bucharest on 5-8 July 1966, the political leaders of the seven active members of the Warsaw Pact (Albania still being excluded) adopted a « Declaration on Strengthening Peace and Security in Europe ». The Declaration, reproduced here in abridged form, calls for a conference of European states to discuss European security.

The People's Republic of Bulgaria, the Czechoslovak Socialist Republic, the Hungarian People's Republic, the German Democratic Republic, the Polish People's Republic, the Socialist Republic of Romania and the Union of Soviet Socialist Republics, the states which are parties to the Warsaw Treaty of Friendship, Cooperation and Mutual Assistance, represented at the meeting in Bucharest of the political consultative committee, adopt the following Declaration:

The safeguarding of a lasting peace and of security in Europe is in accord with the ardent desires of all peoples of the continent of Europe and is in the interests of universal peace...

Now, two decades after the end of World War II, its consequences in Europe have not yet been liquidated, there is no German peace treaty and hotbeds of tension and abnormal situations in relations between states continue to exist.

The socialist states which signed the present Declaration believe that the elimination of this situation and the creation of firm foundations of peace and security in

Europe assume that international relations proceeding from the renunciation of the threat of force or the use of force, and the need to settle international disputes only by peaceful means, should be based on the principles of sovereignty and national independence, equality and non-interference in domestic affairs and on respect of territorial inviolability.

The states of Europe should strive for the adoption of effective measures to prevent the danger of the start of an armed conflict in Europe and for the strengthening of European collective security...

The growth of the forces which are coming out for the preservation and strengthening of peace is one of the determining features of the present international situation...

Tendencies towards getting rid of the features of the cold war and the obstacles standing in the way of a normal development of European co-operation, for the settlement of outstanding issues through mutual understanding, for the normalization of international life and the rapprochement of peoples are increasingly appearing and developing in Europe. This course is opposed by imperialist reactionary circles which, pursuing aggressive aims, strive to fan tension and to poison relations between the European states.

A direct threat to peace in Europe and to the security of the European peoples is presented by the present policy of the United States of America... The United States interferes in the domestic affairs of other states, violates the sacred right of every people to settle its own destiny, resorts to colonial repressions and armed intervention, hatches plots in various countries of Asia, Africa and Latin America, and everywhere supports reactionary forces and venal régimes that are hated by the peoples. There can be no doubt that the aims of the United States policy in

Europe have nothing in common with the vital interests of the European peoples and the aim of European security.

The American ruling circles would like to impose their on their allies in Western Europe and to make Western Europe an instrument of the United States global policy, which is based on the attempt to stop and even turn back the historic process of the national and social liberation of the peoples. Hence the attempts to involve some West European states in military ventures even in other parts of the world, and Asia in particular.

The United States aggressive circles, which have the support of the reactionary forces of Western Europe, are, with the help of the North Atlantic military bloc and the military machine created by it, trying further to deepen the division of Europe, to keep up the arms race, to increase international tensions and tho impede the establishment and development of normal ties between the West European and East European states...

The US policy in Europe, promoted during the post-war years, is the more dangerous for the European peoples in that it is increasingly based on collusion with the militaristic and revanchist forces of West Germany. These forces are openly pushing the United States to promote an even more dangerous course in Europe. This policy is reflected in the projected creation of a sort of alliance between the American imperialists and the West German revanchists.

The militaristic and revanchist circles of West Germany do not want to take the vital interests of the German people itself into account; they are pursuing aggressive aims which manifest themselves in all their actions—in the switching of the country's economic potential to military lines, in the creation of a Bundeswehr of 500,000 men, in the glorification of the history of German conquests and

139

in the nurturing of hatred towards other peoples whose lands are again being covered by these circles in the Federal Republic of Germany.

At present the demand for the possession of nuclear weapons is the focal point of this policy. The creation in the Federal Republic of Germany of a scientific technical and industrial basis that would serve at a certain moment for the manufacture of their own atomic and nuclear bombs is being openly and secretly accelerated. By their joint efforts, the peace-loving countries and peoples have so far succeeded in delaying the creation of a NATO joint nuclear force which would give the Federal Republic of Germany access to nuclear weapons; but the plans for this have not been shelved.

The fundamental interests of all the peoples demand the renunciation of the plans for creating a NATO multi-laterl nuclear force. If, however, the NATO countries, acting contrary to the interests of peace, embark on a course of implementing the plans for creating a multilateral nuclear force or giving West Germany access to nuclear weapons in any form whatsoever, the member states of the Warsaw Treaty Organization would be compelled to carry out the defensive measures necessary to ensure their security.

The territorial claims of the West German revanchists must be emphatically rejected. They are absolutely without basis or prospects. The question of European frontiers has been solved finally and irrevocably. The inviolability of the existing frontiers between European states, including the frontiers of the sovereign German Democratic Republic, Poland and Czechoslovakia, is one of the main prerequisites for ensuring European security.

The states represented at the present meeting confirm their resolution to crush any aggression against them on the part of the forces of imperialism and reaction. For

their part, the member states of the Warsaw Treaty Orgaz-
ation declare that they have no territorial claims whatever
against a single state in Europe. The policy of revanchism
and militarism, carried through by German imperialism,
has always ended in fiasco. Given the present balance of
forces in the world arena and in Europe, it is attended
by irreparable consequences for the Federal Republic of
Germany.

The interests of peace and security in Europe and
throughout the world, like the interests of the German
people, demand that the ruling circles of the Federal
Republic of Germany take the real state of affairs in
Europe into account, and this means that they take as
their point of departure the existence of two German
states, abandon their claims for the frontiers of Europe to
be carved up again, abandon their claims to the right
exclusively to represent the whole of Germany and their
attempts to bring pressure to bear on states that recognize
the German Democratic Republic, renounce the criminal
Munich diktat, and acknowledge that it has been null
and void from the very beginning. They must prove by
deeds that they have really learned the lessons of history
and that the will put an end to militarism and revanchism
and will carry through a policy of the normalization of
relations between states and the development of cooperation and friendship between peoples.

The German Democratic Republic, which is a major
factor making for the safeguarding of peace in Europe,
has addressed the government and Bundestag of the
Federal Republic of Germany with constructive proposals:
to renounce nuclear arms on a reciprocal basis, to reduce
the armies of both German states, to assume a commitment not to use force against each other and to sit down
at a conference table for a solution of the national prob-

lems of interest to both the German Democratic Republic and the Federal Republic of Germany which have developed. The government of the Federal Republic of Germany, however, evinces no interest in these proposals. The states which have signed this Declaration support this initiative of the German Democratic Republic.

Having examined all aspects of the present situation in Europe, the states represented at the meeting have drawn the conclusion that in Europe, where almost half the states are socialist, it is possible to prevent undesirable developments. The problem of European security can be solved by the joint efforts of the European states and all the public forces that are coming out for peace, irrespective of their ideological views and religious or other convictions. This task will be all the more successfully accomplished, the sooner the influence of those forces who would like to continue aggravating tension in the relations between European states is paralyzed...

A major factor which increasingly complicates the carrying out of war gambles in Europe is the growth of the influence of these forces in the West European states which are aware of the need to rise above differences in political views and convictions and come out for a relaxation of international tension, for the comprehensive development of mutually advantageous relations between all the states of Europe without discrimination and for the complete independence of their countries and the maintenance of their national identity.

The states which have signed this Declaration note as a positive feature the presence of circles in the Federal Republic of Germany that come out against revanchism and militarism, which call for the establishment of normal relations with the countries of both the West and the East, including normal relations between both German states, and are pressing for a relaxation of international tension and the safeguarding of European security so that all Germans may enjoy the blessing of peace...

The states that are signatories to this Declaration hold that measures for the strengthening of security in Europe can and should be taken, in the first instance, in the following main directions:

1. They call upon all European states to develop good-neighbourly relations on the basis of the principles of independence and national sovereignty, equality, non-interference in internal affairs and mutual advantage founded on the principles of peaceful co-existence between states with different social systems. Proceeding from this, they come out for the strengthening of economic and trade relations, the multiplication of contacts and forms of co-operation in science, technology, culture and art, as well as in other areas which provide new opportunities for co-operation among European countries...

The development of general European co-operation makes it necessary for all states to renounce any kind of discrimination and pressure, either political or economic in nature, designed against other countries, and requires their equal co-operation and the establishment of normal relations between them, including the establishment of normal relations with both German states. The establishment and development of good-neighbourly relations between European states with different social systems can make their economic and cultural contacts more active and thus increase the possibilities for European states to make an effective contribution to improving the climate in Europe and the development of mutual confidence and respect.

2. The socialist countries have alaways and consist-ently come out against the division of the world into military blocs or alliances, and for the elimination of the dangers which flow from for universal peace and security. The Warsaw Treaty of Friedship, Co-operation and Mutual Assistance—a defensive pact of sovereign and equal states —was concluded in reply to the formation of the military aggressive NATO alignment and the inclusion of West Germany into it. However, the member states of the Warsaw Treaty Organization have considered and consider now that the existence of military blocs and war bases on the territories of other states, which are imposed by the imperialist forces, constitute an obstacle along the road of co-operation between states.

A genuine guarantee of the security and progress of every European country must be the establishment of an effective security system in Europe, based on relations of equality and mutual respect between all states of the continent and on the joint efforts of all European nations —and not the existence of military alignments which do not conform with healthy tendencies in international affairs today. The countries that have signed this Declaration consider that the need has matured for steps to be taken towards the relaxation, above all, of military tension in Europe.

The governments of our states have more than once pointed out that in case of the discontinuance of the oper-ation of the North Atlantic Alliance, the Warsaw Treaty would become invalid, and that their place ought to be taken by a European security system. They now solemnly reaffirm their readiness for the simultaneous abolition of these alliances.

If, however, the member states of the North Atlantic Treaty are still not ready to accept the complete dissolution of both alignments, the states that have signed this Declaration consider that it is already now expedient to reach an understanding on the abolition of the military organization, both of the North Atlantic Pact and of the Warsaw Treaty. At the same time, they declare that as long as the North Atlantic bloc exists, and aggressive imperialist circles encroach on world peace, the socialist countries represented at this meeting, maintaining high vigilance, are fully resolved to strengthen their might and defence potential. At the same time, we believe it necessary that all member states of the North Atlantic Pact and the Warsaw Treaty, and also the countries who do not participate in any military alliances, should exert efforts on a bilateral or multilateral basis with the object of advancing the cause of European security.

3. Great importance is now also assumed by such partial measures towards military relaxation on the European continent as the abolition of foreign war bases; the withdrawal of all forces from foreign territories to within their national frontiers; the reduction, on an agreed scale and at agreed deadlines, of the numerical strength of the armed forces of both German states; measures aimed at eliminating the danger of a nuclear conflict (the setting up of nuclear-free zones and the assumption of the commitment by the nuclear powers not to use these weapons against the states which are parties to such zones, etc.); and the ending of flights by foreign planes carrying atom or hydrogen bombs over the territories of European states and of the entry of foreign submarines and surface ships with nuclear arms on board into the ports of such states.

4. The states must concentrate their efforts on excluding the possibility of access of the Federal Republic

of Germany to nuclear weapons in any form—directly, or indirectly through alignments of states—and to exclusive control or any form of participation in the control of such weapons. The way this problem is resolved will largely determine the future of the peoples of Europe, and not only the peoples of Europe. On this question, too, half-hearted decisions are impermissible.

5. The immutability of frontiers is the foundation of a lasting peace in Europe. The interests of the normalization of the situation in Europe demand that all states, both in Europe and outside the European continent, proceed in their foreign political action from recognition of the frontiers that really exist between European states, including the Polish frontier on the Oder-Neisse line and the frontiers between the two German states.

6. A German peace settlement is in accord with the interests of peace in Europe. The socialist states which are represented at the meeting are ready to continue the search for the solution of this problem. This solution must take into consideration the interests of the security of all the countries concerned and the security of Europe as a whole.

A constructive approach to this question is only possible if it proceeds from reality, above all, from recognition of the fact of the existence of two German states—the German Democratic Republic and the Federal Republic of Germany. At the same time, such a settlement requires recognition of the existing frontiers and the refusal of both German states to possess nuclear weapons...

As for the reunion of both German states, the way to this lies through the relaxation of tension, through a gradual rapprochement between the two sovereign German states and agreements between them, through agreements on disarmament in Germany and Europe, and on the basis of the principle that when Germany is reunited, the united German state would be truly peaceful and democratic and would never again be a danger to its neighbours or to peace in Europe.

7. Convocation of a general European conference to discuss the questions of ensuring security in Europe and organizing general European co-operation would be of great positive importance. The agreement reached at the conference could be expressed, for example, in the form of a general European declaration on co-operation for the maintenance and strengthening of European security. Such a declaration could provide for an undertaking by the signatories to be guided in their relations by the interests of peace, to settle disputes by peaceful means only, to hold consultations and exchange information on question of mutual interest and to contribute to the all-round development of economic, scientific, technical and cultural relations. The declaration should be open to all interested states to join.

The convocation of a conference on questions of European security and co-operation could contribute to the establishment of a system of collective security in Europe and would be an important landmark in the contemporary history of Europe. Our countries are ready to take part in such a conference at any time convenient to the other interested states, both members of the North Atlantic Treaty and neutrals. Neutral European countries could also play a positive rôle in the convocation of such a meeting. It goes without saying that the agenda and other questions concerning the preparation of such a meeting or conference should be decided upon by all participating states together, bearing in mind the proposals submitted by every one of them.

The countries represented at this meeting are also prepared to use other methods available for discussing problems of European security: talks through diplomatic channels, meetings of Foreign Ministers or special representative on a bilateral or multilateral basis and contacts at the highest level. They consider that the considerations above cover the principal, the most important, aspects of ensuring European security. They are also ready to discuss other proposals which have been submitted, or may be submitted by any state, for the solution of this problem... The parties to this meeting are convinced that countries on the other continents, too, cannot be indifferent to how things develop in Europe.

DECLARATION
ON THE FUTURE TASKS OF THE ALLIANCE

Report of the Council

A year ago, on the initiative of the Foreign Minister of Belgium, the governments of the fifteen nations of the Alliance resolved to « study the future tasks which face the Alliance, and its procedures for fulfilling them in order to strengthen the Alliance as a factor for durable peace ». The present report sets forth the general tenor and main principles emerging from this examination of the future tasks of the Alliance.

2. Studies were undertaken by Messrs. Schütz, Watson, Spaak, Kohler and Patijn. The Council wishes to express its appreciation and thanks to these eminent personalities for their efforts and for the analyses they produced.

3. The exercise has shown that the Alliance is a dynamic and vigorous organization which is constantly adapting itself to changing conditions. It also has shown that its future tasks can be handled within the terms of the Treaty by building on the methods and procedures which have proved their value over many years.

4. Since the North Atlantic Treaty was signed in 1949 the international situation has changed significantly and the political tasks of the Alliance have assumed a new

dimension. Amongst other developments, the Alliance has played a major part in stopping Communist expansion in Europe; the USSR has become one of the two world super powers but the Communist world is no longer monolithic; the Soviet doctrine of « peaceful co-existence » has changed the nature of the confrontation with the West but not the basic problems. Although the disparity between the power of the United States and that of the European states remains, Europe has recovered and is on its way towards unity. The process of decolonisation has transformed European relations with the rest of the world; at the same time, major problems have arisen in the relations between developed and developing countries.

5.   The Atlantic Alliance has two main functions. Its first function is to maintain adequate military strength and political solidarity to deter aggression and other forms of pressure and to defend the territory of member countries if aggression should occur. Since its inception, the Alliance has successfully fulfilled this task. But the possibility of a crisis cannot be excluded as long as the central political issues in Europe, first and foremost the German question, remain unsolved. Moreover, the situation of instability and uncertainty still precludes a balanced reduction of military forces. Under these conditions, the Allies will maintain as necessary, a suitable military capability to assure the balance of forces, thereby creating a climate of stability, security and confidence.

In this climate the Alliance can carry out its second function, to pursue the search for progress towards a more stable relationship in which the underlying political issues can be solved. Military security and a policy of detente are not contradictory but complementary. Collective defence is a stabilising factor in world politics. It is the necessary condition for effective policies directed towards a greater relaxation of tensions. The way to peace and stability in Europe rests in particular on the use of the Alliance constructively in the interest of detente. The participation of the USSR and the USA will be necessary to achieve a settlement of the political problems in Europe.

6. From the beginning the Atlantic Alliance has been a co-operative grouping of states sharing the same ideals and with a high degree of common interest. Their cohesion and solidarity provide an element of stability within the Atlantic area.

7. As sovereign states the Allies are not obliged to subordinate their policies to collective decision. The Alliance affords an effective forum and clearing house for the exchange of information and views; thus, each of the Allies can decide its policy in the light of close knowledge of the problems and objectives of the others. To this end the practice of frank and timely consultations needs to be deepened and improved. Each Ally should play its full part in promoting an improvement in relations with the Soviet Union and the countries of Eastern Europe, bearing in mind that the pursuit of detente must not be allowed to split the Alliance. The chances of success will clearly be greatest if the Allies remain on parallel courses, especially in matters of close concern to them all; their actions will thus be all the more effective.

8. No peaceful order in Europe is possible without a major effort by all concerned. The evolution of Soviet and East European policies gives ground for hope that those governments may eventually come to recognise the advan-

tages to them of collaborating in working towards a peaceful settlement. But no final and stable settlement in Europe is possible without a solution of the German question which lies at the heart of present tensions in Europe. Any such settlement must end the unnatural barriers between Eastern and Western Europe, which are most clearly and cruelly manifested in the division of Germany.

9. Accordingly the Allies are resolved to direct their energies to this purpose by realistic measures designed to further a detente in East-West relations. The relaxation of tensions is not the final goal but is part of a long-term process to promote better relations and to foster a European settlement. The ultimate political purpose of the Alliance is to achieve a just and lasting peaceful order in Europe accompanied by appropriate security guarantees.

10. Currently, the development of contacts between the countries of Western and Eastern Europe is mainly on a bilateral basis. Certain subjects, of course, require by their very nature a multilateral solution.

11. The problem of German reunification and its relationship to a European settlement has normally been dealt with in exchanges between the Soviet Union and the three Western powers having special responsibilities in this field. In the preparation of such exchanges the Federal Republic of Germany has regularly joined the three Western powers in order to reach a common position. The other Allies will continue to have their views considered in timely discussions among the Allies about Western policy on this subject, without in any way impairing the special responsibilities in question.

12. The Allies will examine and review suitable policies designed to achieve a just and stable order in Europe, to overcome the division of Germany and to foster European security. This will be part of a process of active and constant preparation for the time when fruitful discussions of these complex questions may be possible bilaterally or multilaterally between Eastern and Western nations.

13. The Allies are studying disarmament and practical arms control measures, including the possibility of balanced force reductions. These studies will be intensified. Their active pursuit reflects the will of the Allies to work for an effective detente with the East.

14. The Allies will examine with particular attention the defence problems of the exposed areas e.g. the South-Eastern flank. In this respect the present situation in the Mediterranean presents special problems, bearing in mind that the current crisis in the Middle East falls within the responsibilities of the United Nations.

15. The North Atlantic Treaty area cannot be treated in isolation from the rest of the world. Crises and conflicts arising outside the area may impair its security either directly or by affecting the global balance. Allied countries contribute individually within the United Nations and other international organisations to the maintenance of international peace and security and to the solution of important international problems. In accordance with established usage the Allies or such of them as wish to do so will also continue to consult on such problems without commitment and as the case may demand.

16. In the light of these findings, the Ministers directed the Council in permanent session to carry out, in the

years ahead, the detailed follow-up resulting from this study. This will be done either by intensifying work already in hand or by activating highly specialized studies by more systematic use of experts and officials sent from capitals.

17. Ministers found that the study by the Special Group confirmed the importance of the role which the Alliance is called upon to play during the coming years in the promotion of detente and the strengthening of peace. Since significant problems have not yet been examined in all their aspects, and other problems of no less significance which have arisen from the latest political and strategic developments have still to be examined, the Ministers have directed the Permanent Representatives to put in hand the study of these problems without delay, following such procedures as shall be deemed most appropriate by the Council in permanent session, in order to enable further reports to be subsequently submitted to the Council in Ministerial Session.

MUTUAL AND BALANCED FORCE REDUCTIONS

Declaration Adopted by Foreign Ministers and Representatives of Countries Participating in the NATO Defence Programme

1.   Meeting at Reykjavik on 24th and 25th June, 1968, the Ministers recalled the frequently expressed and strong desire of their countries to make progress in the field of disarmament and arms control.

2.   Ministers recognized that the unresolved issues which still divide the European Continent must be settled by peaceful means, and are convinced that the ultimate goal of a lasting, peaceful order in Europe requires an atmosphere of trust and confidence and can only be reached by a step-by-step process. Mindful of the obvious and considerable interest of all European States in this goal, Ministers expressed their belief that measures in this field including balanced and mutual force reductions can contribute significantly to the lessening of tension and to further reducing the danger of war.

3.   Ministers noted the important work undertaken within the North Atlantic Council by member governments in examining possible proposals for such reductions pursuant to paragraph 13 of the "Report on the Future Tasks of the Alliance", approved by the Ministers in December 1967. In particular, they have taken note of the work being done in the Committee of Political Advisers to establish bases of comparison and to analyse alternative

ways of achieving a balanced reduction of forces, particularly in the Central part of Europe.

4. Ministers affirmed the need for the Alliance to maintain an effective military capability and to assure a balance of forces between NATO and the Warsaw Pact. Since the security of the NATO countries and the prospects for mutual force reductions would be weakened by NATO reductions alone, Ministers affirmed the proposition that the overall military capability of NATO should not be reduced except as part of a pattern of mutual force reductions balanced in scope and timing.

5. Accordingly, Ministers directed Permanent Representatives to continue and intensify their work in accordance with the following agreed principles:

(a) Mutual force reductions should be reciprocal and balanced in scope and timing.

(b) Mutual reductions should represent a substantial and significant step, which will serve to maintain the present degree of security at reduced cost, but should not be such as to risk de-stabilizing the situation in Europe.

(c) Mutual reductions should be consonant with the aim of creating confidence in Europe generally and in the case of each party concerned.

(d) To this end, any new arrangement regarding forces should be consistent with the vital security interests of all parties and capable of being carried out effectively.

6. Ministers affirmed the readiness of their governments to explore with other interested states specific and practical steps in the arms control field.

7. In particular, Ministers agreed that it was desirable that a process leading to mutual force reductions should be initiated. To that end they decided to make all necessary preparations for discussions on this subject with the Soviet Union and other countries of Eastern Europe and they call on them to join in this search for progress towards peace.

8. Ministers directed their Permanent Representatives to follow up on this declaration.

ADDRESS BY WARSAW PACT MEMBER COUNTRIES TO ALL EUROPEAN COUNTRIES

The People's Republic of Bulgaria, the Hungarian People's Republic, the German Democratic Republic, the Polish People's Republic, the Socialist Republic of Rumania, the Union of Soviet Socialist Republics and the Czechoslovak Socialist Republic, the Warsaw Treaty member countries, participants in the Meetings of the Political Consultative Committee, expressing the aspirations of their peoples to live in peace and good neighbourhood with the other European peoples, and also their firm resolve to facilitate the establishment of an atmosphere of security and cooperation on our continent, address all European states with the following call to redouble their efforts aimed at strengthening peace and security in Europe.

The present and future of the peoples of Europe cannot be divorced from the maintenance and consolidation of peace on our continent. Genuine security and reliable peace can be safeguarded if the thoughts, deeds and energies of the European states are aimed at the relaxation of tension the solution of matured international problems, taking account of reality, and the establishment of allround cooperation on a general-European foundation.

The road to good neighbourhood, confidence and mutual understanding depends on the will and efforts of the peoples and governments of all European countries. Contemporary Europe, as it emerged from World War Two, means over 30 states, large and small, differing in their social order, location and interests. By the will of history, they were fated to live side by side, and no one can change this fact.

Ever more governments, parliaments, parties, political leaders and public figures are becoming aware of the responsibility they bear before the present and future generations to prevent another military conflict in Europe. However, forces also continue operating in Europe which regard as assets of European development not the settlement of disputes and peaceful agreements, but additional divisions and missiles, fresh military programmes, designed for decades ahead. Together with them also operate those who have not learnt the appropriate lessons from the outcome of World War Two, as a result of which German militarism and nazism routed. Their intrigues are a source of tension and complicate international relations.

The states, participants in the Meeting, regard it as their duty to continue doing their utmost to protect Europe from the danger of new military conflicts, to open wide scope for the development of cooperation between all European countries, irrespective of their social order, on the basis of the principles of peaceful coexistence.

No matter how intricate the outstanding problems are, they must be solved peacefully through talks, and not through the use of force or the threat of its use.

Analysing the situation in Europe, the Warsaw Treaty member-countries consider that there are real opportunities of safeguarding European security through common efforts, taking into account the interests of all states and peoples of Europe.

Almost three years ago, the Warsaw Treaty member-countries, in Bucharest advanced a proposal for the convocation of a General-European Conference to discuss problems of European security and peaceful cooperation. Contacts maintained since that time have shown that not a single European government has opposed the idea of a General-European Conference and that there are real possibilities of holding it.

After World War Two the states of Europe have not yet met all together even once, though there are many questions which wait for their discussion at a conference table. If one proceeds from the interests of strengthening peace, there are no weighty reasons whatever for postponing the convocation of a General-European Conference.

Such a Conference would accord with the interests of all European states. It would make it possible together to find ways and means which would lead to the liquidation of the division of Europe into military alignments and to the realisation of peaceful cooperation between the European states and peoples.

However, there are forces in the world which, seeking to maintain the division of our continent, pursuing a policy of fanning tensions, and refusing the establishment of peaceful cooperation between states and peoples, oppose the convocation of such a Conference and other steps to strengthen European security.

The states, participants in this Meeting, are convinced that the development of general-European cooperation has been and remains the only real alternative to the dangerous military confrontation, the arms race, the dissensions, which the aggressive forces, seeking to explode the results of World War Two and to recarve the map of Europe, try to continue imposing upon Europe.

The Warsaw Treaty member-countries reaffirm their proposals spearheaded against the division of the world into military blocs, the arms race and the threats emanating from this for the cause of peace and security of the peoples, and the other steps and provisions, contained in

160

the Declaration on the strengthening of peace and security in Europe, adopted in Bucharest in 1966.

It is a vital need for the European peoples to avert fresh military conflicts, to strengthen political, economic and cultural contacts between all states on the basis of equality, respect for the independence and sovereignty of states. A firm system of European security will create an objective possibility and necessity of implementing through joint efforts major projects in power engineering, transport, water and air basin, health services, which have a direct bearing on the welfare of the population of all the continent. It is precisely this common factor that can and must become a foundation of European cooperation.

One of the main preconditions of safeguarding European security is the inviolability of the frontiers existing in Europe, including the frontiers on the Oder and Neisse and also the frontiers between the German Democratic Republic and the Federal Republic of Germany, recognition of the existence of the GDR and the FRG, renunciation by the Federal Republic of Germany of its claims to represent the entire German people, renunciation of the possession of nuclear weapons in any shape. West Berlin has a special status and does not belong to West Germany.

A practical step towards strengthening European security would be the earliest possible meeting of representatives of all interested European states to establish by mutual consent both the procedure for the convocation of the Conference and the definition of the items on its agenda. We are ready to consider at the same time any other proposal for the method of preparing and convening this Conference.

The states, participants in the Meeting of the Political Consultative Committee, address all countries of Europe with the call for cooperation in convening a General

European Conference and creating the necessary pre-conditions so that this Conference could be successful and justify the hopes pinned upon it by the peoples.

For the implementation of this important action, which would be a historic moment in the life of the continent, the states, participants in the Meeting, address all European countries with the solemn call to strengthen the climate of confidence and, with this object in view, to refrain from any actions, which could poison the atmosphere in the relations between states. They address the call to pass over from common statements on peace to specific actions and steps of detente and disarmament, they call for the development of cooperation and peace between the peoples. They address all European governments with the call to pool their efforts so that Europe become a continent of fruitful cooperation between equal nations, a factor of stability, peace and mutual understanding throughout the world.

DECLARATION OF THE CONSULTATIVE MEETING OF THE MINISTERS OF FOREIGN AFFAIRS OF THE WARSAW PACT MEMBER STATES

On October 30 and 31, 1969, consultations took place in Prague of the Ministers of Foreign Affairs of the member states of the Warsaw Pact.

The governments represented at the consultations emphasized their efforts and willingness to undertake individually or in co-operation with other states new steps aims at the relaxation of tension, strengthening of security and development of peaceful co-operation in Europe. They reaffirm the provisions of the Budapest appeal of the participating Warsaw Treaty states to all European countries of March 17, 1969, which have proved their vitality.

The participants in the consultations paid special attention to the preparations for the covening of the all-European conference on the questions of security and co-operation in Europe. They noted with satisfaction that the proposal for the holding of the European conference has met with a positive response on the part of most European states. In Europe the proposal has become a subject of active—and matter of fact consideration, in the course of which concrete ideas were advanced in regard of various questions relating to the preparation of the conference. This creates practical possibilities for the covering of the conference and for the achievement of European security through joint efforts in the interest of all states and people of Europe.

The valuable initiative taken by the Finnish government on May 5, 1969, whereby it declared its willingness to assist in the preparation and holding of the all-European conference, was also welcomed with appreciations. All countries-signataries of the Budapest appeal responded in a positive manner.

The Ministers of Foreign Affairs of the Warsaw Treaty member states, acting on instructions of their governments, propose that the following questions should be included in the agenda of the all-European conference:

1. the ensuring of European security and renunciation of the use of force or threat of its use in the mutual relations among states in Europe;

2. expansion of trade, economic, scientific and technical relations on the principle of equal rights, aimed at the development of political co-operation among European states.

The socialist states which signed this declaration are deeply convinced that a fruithful consideration of the above mentioned questions and the reaching of agreement in that respect would facilitate a lessening of tension in Europe, growth of a mutual understanding, development of peaceful and friendly relations among states, and thereby the ensuring of security in which all European states are vitally interested. The success of the all-European conference would constitute a historic event in the life of our continent and in the life of the nations all over the world. It would open up a way to the subsequent consideration of other problems of interest to European states, whose solution would correspond with the strengthening of peace in Europe, assist in the development of broad mutually beneficial co-operation among all European states, and the ensuring of reliable security based on collective principles and joint efforts of the states par-

164

ticipants in the all-European conference in Europe as it has been constituted and exists today.

The governments participants in these consultations propose that those views should be discussed within the framework of the preparatory work preceding the all-European conference in the course of bilateral or multilateral consultations among interested states. They are of course willing to discuss any other suggestions aimed at the practical preparation and ensuring of the success of the all-European conference.

The Ministers of Foreign Affairs express on behalf of their governments the conviction that in spite of certain still unresolved difficulties all issues pertaining to the preparation and holding of the all-European conference, whether they concern the agenda, range of participants or manner of covening the conference, might be settled, provided good will and sincere endeavour to achieve mutual understanding are shown.

The governments of the Bulgarian People's Republic, Hungarian People's Republic, German Democratic Republic, Polish People's Republic, Rumanian Socialist Republic call upon all European states to strive in the interest of the continent's peaceful future for a speeder convening of the all-European conference which might in their opinion be held in Helsinki in the first half of 1970.

DECLARATION OF THE NORTH
ATLANTIC COUNCIL

1. Meeting at Brussels on 4th and 5th December, 1969, the Ministers of the North Atlantic Alliance reaffirmed the commitment of their nations to pursue effective policies directed towards a greater relaxation of tensions in their continuing search for a just and durable peace.

2. Peace and security in Europe must rest upon universal respect for the principles of sovereign equality, political independence and the territorial integrity of each European state; the right of its peoples to shape their own destinies; the peaceful settlement of disputes; non-intervention in the internal affairs of any state by any other state, whatever their political or social system; and the renunciation of the use or the threat of force against any state. Past experience has shown that there is, as yet, no common interpretation of these principles. The fundamental problems in Europe can be solved only on the basis of these principles and any real and lasting improvement of East-West relations presupposes respect for them without any conditions or reservations.

3. At their meeting in Washington in April 1969, Ministers had expressed the intention of their governments to explore with the Soviet Union and the other countries of Eastern Europe which concrete issues best lend themselves to fruitful negotiation and an early resolution. To this end, the Council has been engaged in a detailed study of various issues for exploration and possible negotiation.

Ministers recognized that procedure merited closer examination and, accordingly, requested the Council in Permanent Session to report to the next Ministerial Meeting.

4. Ministers considered that, in an era of negotiation, it should be possible, by means of discussion of specific and well-defined subjects, progressively to reduce tensions. This would in itself facilitate discussion of the more fundamental questions.

Arm Control and Disarmament

5. Ministers again expressed the interest of the Alliance in arms control and disarmament and recalled the Declaration on mutual and balanced force reductions adopted at Reykjavik in 1968 and reaffirmed in Washington in 1969. The Members of the Alliance have noted that up to now this suggestion has led to no result. The Allies, nevertheless, have continued, and will continue, their studies in order to prepare a realistic basis for active exploration at an early date and thereby establish whether it could serve as a starting point for fruitful negotiations. They requested that a report of the Council in Permanent Session on the preparation of models for mutual and balanced force reductions be submitted as soon as possible.

6. Ministers of countries participating in NATO's integrated defence programme consider that the studies on mutual and balanced force reductions have progressed sufficiently to permit the establishment of certain criteria which, in their view, such reductions should meet. Significant reductions under adequate verification and control would be envisaged under any agreement on mutual and

167

balanced force reductions, which should also be consistent with the vital security interests of all parties. This would be another concrete step in advancing « along the road of ending the arms race and of general and complete disarmament, including nuclear disarmament ».

7. These Ministers directed that further studies be given to measures which could accompany or follow agreement on mutual and balanced force reductions. Such measures could include advance notification of military movements and manœuvres, exchange of observers at military manœuvres and possibly the establishment of observation posts. Examination of the techniques and methods of inspection should also be further developed.

Germany and Berlin

8. The Ministers welcome the efforts of the governments of the United States, Great Britain, and France, in the framework of their special responsibility for Berlin and Germany as a whole, to gain the co-operation of the Soviet Union in improving the situation with respect to Berlin and free access to the city. The elimination of difficulties created in the past with respect to Berlin, especially with regard to access, would increase the prospects for serious discussions on the other concrete issues which continue to divide East and West. Furthermore, Berlin could play a constructive role in the expansion of East-West economic relations if the city's trade with the East could be facilitated.

9. A just and lasting peace settlement for Germany must be based on the free decision of the German people and on the interests of European security. The Ministers

are convinced that, pending such a settlement, the proposals of the Federal Republic for a modus vivendi between the two parts of Germany and for a bilateral exchange of declarations on the non-use of force or the threat of force would, if they receive a positive response, substantially facilitate co-operation between East and West on other problems. They consider that these efforts by the Federal Republic represent constructive steps toward relaxation of tension in Europe and express the hope that the governments will therefore take them into account in forming their own attitude toward the German question.

10. The Ministers would regard concrete progress in both these fields as an important contribution to peace in Europe. They are bound to attach great weight to the responses to these proposals in evaluating the prospects for negotiations looking toward improved relations and co-operation in Europe.

Economic, technical and cultural exchanges

11. Allied governments consider that not only economic and technical but also cultural exchanges between interested countries can bring mutual benefit and understanding. In these fields more could be achieved by freer movement of people, ideas, and information between the countries of East and West.

12. The benefit of the Alliance's work in the field of human environment would be enhanced if it were to become the basis of broader co-operation. This could, and should, be an early objective, being one in which the Warsaw Pact governments have indicated an interest.

Further co-operation could also be undertaken, for example, in the more specialised field of oceanography. More intensive efforts in such fields should be pursued either bilaterally, multilaterally or in the framework of existing international bodies comprising interested countries.

Perspectives for negotiations

13. The Ministers considered that the concrete issues concerning European security and co-operation mentioned in this Declaration are subjects lending themselves to possible discussions or negotiations with the Soviet Union and the other countries of Eastern Europe. The Allied governments will continue and intensify their contacts, discussions or negotiations through all appropriate channels, bilateral or multilateral, believing that progress is most likely to be achieved by choosing in each instance the means most suitable for the subject. Ministers therefore expressed their support for bilateral initiatives undertaken by the German Federal Government with the Soviet Union and other countries of Eastern Europe, looking toward agreements on the renunciation of force and the threat of force. Ministers expressed the hope that existing contacts will be developed so as to enable all countries concerned to participate in discussions and negotiations on substantial problems of co-operation and security in Europe with real prospects of success.

DECLARATION ON MUTUAL
AND BALANCED FORCE REDUCTIONS

1. Meeting at Rome on 26th and 27th May, 1970, the Ministers representing countries participating in NATO's Integrated Defence Programme recall and reaffirm the commitment of their nations to pursue effective policies directed towards a greater relaxation of tensions in their continuing search for a just and durable peace. They recall, in particular, the invitations they have previously addressed to the Soviet Union and other countries of Eastern Europe to join them in discussing the possibility of mutual and balanced force reductions.

2. The objective of the work on which their representatives have been engaged has been to prepare a realistic basis for active explorations between the interested parties at an early date and thereby to establish whether it could serve as a starting point for fruitful negotiation. Such exploratory talks would assist those concerned in developing in detail criteria and objectives for substantive negotiations to follow at the appropriate stage in a forum to be determined. They would also provide tangible evidence of the readiness to build confidence between East and West.

3. Ministers invite interested states to hold exploratory talks on mutual and balanced force reductions in Europe, with special reference to the Central Region. They agree that in such talks the Allies would put forward the following considerations:

(a) Mutual force reductions should be compatible with the vital security interests of the Alliance and should not operate to the military disadvantage of either side having regard for the differences arising from geographical and other considerations.

(b) Reductions should be on a basis of reciprocity, and phased and balanced as to their scope and timing.

(c) Reductions should include stationed and indigenous forces and their weapons systems in the area concerned.

(d) There must be adequate verification and controls to ensure the observance of agreements on mutual and balanced force reductions.

4. As a first step Ministers requested the Foreign Minister of Italy to transmit this Declaration on their behalf through diplomatic channels to all other interested parties, including neutral and nonaligned governments. They further agreed that in the course of their normal bilateral and other contacts member governments would seek to obtain the responses and reactions of other governments. Members of the Alliance will consult further regarding the outcome of their soundings with a view to enabling the Alliance to determine what further individual or joint exploration might be useful.

3rd - 4th December, 1970

Brussels

Chairman: Mr. M. Brosio.

President Nixon's statement regarding US forces in Europe - International situation reviewed - Progress on Berlin and other talks affirmed to be condition of multilateral exploration of European security - Principles governing inter-state relations - MBFR - Environment problems - Co-operation on defence equipment - **DPC** *meeting (2nd December) - Approves Report on defence problems of Alliance in the 1970s - Validity of NATO strategy - NATO Security Indivisible - European defence improvement programme - Mediterranean - Crisis management - Nuclear Affairs.*

Report on defence problems of Alliance in the 1970s annexed to Communiqué.

The North Atlantic Council met in Ministerial Session at Brussels on 3rd and 4th December, 1970. Foreign, Defence and Finance Ministers were present.

2. Ministers again stated that the political purpose of the Alliance is the common search for peace through initiatives aiming at the relaxation of tension and the establishment of a just and lasting peaceful order in Europe, accompanied by appropriate security guarantees.

3. The Council received a statement from President Nixon which pledged that, given a similar approach by

the other Allies, the Unites States would maintain and improve its own forces in Europe and would not reduce them except in the context of reciprocal East-West action. Ministers expressed their profound satisfaction at the reaffirmation of Alliance solidarity expressed in this statement.

4. Ministers reviewed the international situation as it had developed since their last meeting in May in Rome. They noted that 1970 had been a year of extensive diplomatic activity by member goverments of the Alliance to initiate or intensify contacts, discussions and negotiations with the members of the Warsaw Pact and with other European countries. Ministers paid particular attention to the Strategic Arms Limitations Talks, the Treaties negotiated by the Federal Republic of Germany with the Soviet Union and Poland, intra-German relations, Berlin and the situation in the Mediterranean.

5. Ministers welcomed the resumption at Helsinki in November of the negotiations between the United States and the USSR on Strategic Arms Limitations. They expressed the hope that the talks would lead, at an early date, to an agreement strengthening peace and security in Europe and in the world.

6. Ministers noted with satisfaction the signing of the Treaty between the Federal Republic of Germany and the USSR on 12th August, 1970, and the initialling of the Treaty between the Federal Republic of Germany and the Polish People's Republic on 18th November, 1970. They welcomed these Treaties as contributions toward reduction of tensions in Europe and as important elements of the *modus vivendi* which the Federal Republic

of Germany wishes to establish with its Eastern neighbours. Ministers noted the clarifications made in the context of the Treaties, and reflected in the exchanges of notes between the Federal Republic of Germany and the Three Powers, to the effect that quadripartite rights and responsibilities for Berlin and Germany as a whole remain unaffected pending a peace settlement which would be based on the free decision of the German people and on the interests of European security. Ministers welcomed the beginning of an exchange of views between the Federal Republic of Germany and the GDR and expressed the hope that this exchange will prepare the ground for genuine negotiations between the two. Ministers reviewed the development of the quadripartite talks in Berlin.

7. In considering the situation with regard to Berlin and Germany, Ministers recalled their statement in the Brussels Declaration of 5th December, 1969 (paragraph 10) to the effect that concrete progress in both these fields would constitute an important contribution to peace and would have great weight in their evaluation of the prospects for improving East-West relations in Europe. Indeed, these prospects would be put in question the existing ties between the Western sectors of Berlin negotiations. With this in mind, Ministers stressed the importance of securing unhindered access to Berlin, improved circulation within Berlin and respect by all for the existinfi ties between the Western sectors of Berlin and the Federal Republic of Germany which have been established with the approval of the Three Powers. They underlined the need for an understanding between the Federal Republic of Germany and the GDR on a negotiated settlement of their mutual relations which would take account of the special features of the situation in Germany.

8. Ministers took note of a report on the situation in the Mediterranean prepared on their instructions by the Council in Permanent Session. They noted that the evolution of events in the area gives cause for concern and justifies careful vigilance on the part of the Allies. They recommended that consultations on this question should continue, and they invited the Council in Permanent Session to keep the situation under review and to report fully thereon at their next meeting.

9. As a result of their review of the international situation and its positive and negative aspects, Ministers emphasised that these developments in Europe and the Mediterranean all affect the Alliance directly or indirectly, and have a bearing on the possibilities of reducing tensions and promoting peace.

10. Ministers noted that the initiatives which had been taken by Allied Governments had already achieved certain results which constituted some progress in important fields of East-West relations. Nevertheless their hope had been that more substantial progress would have been recorded in bilateral exploratory contacts and in the on-going negotiations, so that active consideration could have been given to the institution of broad multilateral contacts which would deal with the substantial problems of security and co-operation in Europe. They affirmed the readiness of their governments, as soon as the talks on Berlin have reached a satisfactory conclusion and in governments to explore when it would be possible to convene a conference, or a series of conferences, on so far as the other on-going talks are proceeding favourably, to enter into multilateral contacts with all interested security and co-operation in Europe. In this event, the Council would give immediate attention to this question.

176

11. In the meantime, the Council in Permanent Session will continue its study of the results which might be achieved at any such conference or series of conferences, and of the appropriate exploratory and preparatory procedures, including the proposals that have already been advanced. The Allied Governments will also pursue energetically their bilateral exploratory conversations with all interested states on questions affecting security and co-operation.

12. Ministers recalled that any genuine and lasting improvement in East-West relations in Europe must be based on the respect of the following principles which should govern relations between states and which would be included among the points to be explored: sovereign equality, political independence and territorial integrity of each European state; non-interference and non-intervention in the internal affairs of any state, regardless of its political or social system; and the right of the people of each European state to shape their own destinies free of external constraint. A common understanding and application of these principles, without condition or reservation, would give full meaning to any agreement on mutual renunciation of the use or threat of force.

13. In the field of international co-operation, the contacts mentioned in paragraph 10 might provide an opportunity to consider ways and means of ensuring closer co-operation between interested countries on the cultural, economic, technical and scientific levels, and on the question of human environment. Ministers reaffirmed that the freer movement of people, ideas and information is an essential element for the development of such co-operation.

14. Ministers noted that Alliance studies on the various aspects of the mutual and balanced force reductions question have further progressed since the Rome Meeting and instructed the Council in Permanent Session to pursue studies in this field.

15. Ministers representing countries participating in NATO's integrated Defence Programme re-emphasised the importance they attach to mutual and balanced force reductions as a means of reducing tensions and lessening the military confrontation in Europe and recalled the Declarations on this question issued at Reykjavik in 1968 and at Rome earlier this year. They noted that the Warsaw Pact countries have not directly responded to these Declarations but have mentioned the possibility of a discussion at some future time of the question of reducing foreign armed forces on the territory of European states.

16. These Ministers renewed their invitation to interested states to hold exploratory talks on the basis of their Rome Declaration, and also indicated their readiness within this framework to examine different possibilities in the field of force reductions in the Central Region of Europe, including the possible mutual and balanced reduction of stationed forces, as part of an integral programme for the reduction of both stationed and indigenous forces.

17. Ministers reaffirmed their profound interest in genuine disarmament and arms control measures. In this connection, they expressed their satisfaction with progress towards a ban on the emplacement of weapons

of mass destruction on the sea bed. They further considered the pursuit of Allied efforts and studies in all fields related to disarmament to be essential, including those concerning biological and chemical weapons. They invited the Council in Permanent Session to continue to examine these matters.

18. Ministers endorsed the recent Council recommendation to Allied Governments to start work at once in order to achieve, by 1975 if possible but no later than the end of the decade, the elimination of intentional discharger of oil and oily wastes into the sea. This and other accomplishments of the Committee on the Challenges of Modern Society during the past year were welcomed by Ministers as evidence that the Allies are effectively combining their resources to stimulate national and international action on environmental problems.

19. Ministers examined a report on the achievements of the Conference of National Armaments Directors and its subordinate bodies in the promotion of co-operation in research, development and production of military equipment during the four years of its existence. They noted that, in spite of the excellent progress that had been made in the exchange of information on defence equipment, it had proved possible to establish relatively few firm NATO projects for co-operative development and production of equipment. They recognised that more political support would be necessary to overcome the obstacles to greater co-operation. They agreed to the need for a more positive approach in order to achieve the financial and operational benefits of more widespread adoption of jointly developed and produced equipment.

20. Ministers of the countries participating in NATO's integrated defence programme met as the Defence Planning Committee on 2nd December, 1970.

21. Ministers concentrated their discussion on a comprehensive study, which has been in progress since last May, of the defence problems which the Alliance will face in the 1970s. They approved for public release the text at Annex.

22. Ministers confirmed that NATO's approach to security in the 1970s will continue to be based on the twin concepts of defence and detente. They reaffirmed the principle that the overall military capability of NATO should not be reduced except as part of a pattern of mutual force reductions balanced in scope and timing. They agreed that East-West negotiations can be expected to succeed only if NATO maintains an effective deterrent and defensive posture. Ministers confirmed the continued validity of the NATO strategy of flexibility in response, which includes forward defence, reinforcement of the flanks and capabilities for rapid mobilisation, and calls for the maintenance of military capabilities which are able to provide an appropriate counter to any aggression. They noted the continuous rise in Soviet defence and defence-related expenditure and the evidence that the USSR is continuing to strengthen still further its military establishment, including that in the maritime field where Soviet power and the range of its activity have markedly increased. They, therefore, emphasised the need for improvements in NATO's conventional deterrent, as well as the maintenance of a sufficient and modern tactical and strategic nuclear deterrent.

180

23. The security of NATO being indivisible. Ministers underlined the special military and political role of North American forces present in Europe as an irreplaceable contribution to the common defence. In parallel they welcomed the important decision of European member nations participating in NATO's integrated defence programme to make an increased common European effort to strengthen the defence capability of the Alliance. The establishment of a special European Defence Improvement Programme of substantial additional measures will significantly strengthen NATO's capacity for defence and for crisis management in fields, including communications, which have been identified in the "AD 70s" Study as having particular importance.

24. In respect of the above Study, Ministers invited the Defence Planning Committee in Permanent Session to draw up a suitable programme and to ensure that all possible progress is made.

25. Ministers noted the force commitments undertaken by member nations for the year 1971 and adopted the five-year NATO force plan covering the period 1971-1975. They gave directions for the development of a force plan for the next NATO planning period.

26. Ministers viewed with concern the evidence of continuing growth in Soviet military strength in the Mediterranean. Such developments, they felt, could constitute an increasingly significant threat to the security of the Alliance. Ministers commented with approval on steps which have been taken to improve the Alliance's defence posture in the Mediterranean. Referring to their Communique issued in Brussels on 11th June of this

year, Ministers directed that urgent attention be given to the development and implementation of further appropriate measures.

27. Within the field of crisis management, Ministers reviewed communications facilities for high level political consultation and for command and control; they agreed to a number of important measures designed to improve and expand these vital facilities. They encouraged further efforts in the field of civil preparedness and civil emergency planning. They noted progress made on various defence studies. They also noted that the trend towards more sophisticated equipment at increasing cost may well continue, and they stressed that forthcoming modernisation programmes would offer an opportunity for increased co-operation.

28. The Ministerial Meeting also provided the Defence Ministers comprising the Nuclear Defence Affairs Committee (Belgium, Canada, Denmark, Germany, Greece, Italy, Netherlands, Norway, Portugal, Turkey, United Kingdom and United States) with the occasion to review work recently in progress in the Nuclear Planning Group and plans for the future. Acting on the recommendation of the Nuclear Defence Affairs Committee, the Defence Planning Committee adopted the policy documents elaborated by the Nuclear Planning Group at their meeting in Venice last Spring and finalised at Ottawa in October this year. These documents are in consonance with NATO's strategy of flexibility in response.

29. The next Ministerial Meeting of the Defence Planning Committee will take place in the Spring of 1971.

30. The Spring Ministerial Meeting of the Council will be held in Lisbon on 3rd and 4th June, 1971.

31. Ministers requested the Foreign Minister of Belgium to transmit this Communiqué on their behalf through diplomatic channels to all other interested parties including neutral and nonaligned governments.

ALLIANCE DEFENCE FOR THE SEVENTIES

(Annex to the Communique)

The Allied countries participating in the integrated defence efforts decided at a meeting of the Defence Planning Committee in Permanent Session in May of this year to examine in depth NATO defence problems for the next decade.

2. The North Atlantic Alliance has made a practice over the years of periodically conducting major reviews and adapting its policies to accord with the changing circumstances of the times. A notable recent example was the study undertaken in 1967 which resulted in the Report on the Future Tasks of the Alliance establishing defence and detente as complementary pillars of its activities. That Report stated that "collective defence is a stabilising factor in world politics. It is the necessary condition for effective policies directed towards a greater relaxation of tension". Against this background, governments earlier this year recognised the particular timeliness

of a full and candid exchange of views among the Allies on their common defence over the next ten years. This examination of NATO's defence capability in the light of current and prospective military and political developments has now been completed.

3. NATO's approach to security in the 1970s will continue to be based on the twin concepts of defence and detente. Defence problems cannot be seen in isolation but must be viewed in the broader context of the Alliance's basic purpose of ensuring the security of its members. There is a close inter-relationship between the maintenance of adequate defensive strength and the negotiation of settlements affecting the security of the member states.

4. The 1970s could develop into an era of successful negotiations between members of the North Atlantic Alliance and those of the Warsaw Pact. On Western initiative, there are now negotiations under way between East and West which could lead to a real relaxation of tensions. It is hoped that there will be satisfactory progress in on-going talks on a limitation of strategic nuclear weapons and on an improvement of the situation in and around Berlin, and in other current negotiations between individual members of NATO and the Warsaw Pact. The Alliance will continue to seek improved East-West relations, and in the framework of this effort, one of its principal aims will be to engage the Soviet Union and its allies in meaningful talks on mutual and balanced force reductions and other disarmament measures. Progress in this field would facilitate dealing with the defence problems of the next decade. This period might also see convenend one or more conferences on European security and co-operation.

5. On the other hand, the Allies cannot ignore certain disturbing features in the international situation. The evidence thus far suggests that the USSR, intent on extending and strengthening its political power, conducts its international relations on the basis of concepts some of which are not conducive to detente. In particular, its concept of sovereignty is clearly inconsistent with United Nations' principles. At the same time, Soviet military capabilities, besides guaranteeing the USSR's security, continue to increase and provide formidable backing for the wide-ranging assertion of Soviet influence and presence, persistently raising questions regarding their intentions. In real terms, there has been a continuous rise in Soviet defence and defence-related expenditures between 1965 and 1969 of about 5% to 6% per year on average and the evidence is that the USSR is continuing to strengthen its military establishments still further. The contrast between these figures and the corresponding information relating to the Alliance may be seen from paragraph 10 below. Whether East-West relations can in these circumstances be significantly improved will depend mainly on the actions of the USSR and its Warsaw Pact allies, and on the attitudes they bring to negotiations now in progress or in prospect.

6. The position of the Alliance and its member countries during this period of exploration and negotiation, with special reference to European security and mutual force reductions, would be weakened if NATO were to reduce its forces unilaterally, especially those in the European area, and in particular at a time when it is confronted with a steady growth in Soviet military power, which manifests itself above all in the strategic nuclear and maritime fields. NATO member states must, therefore,

maintain a sufficient level of conventional and nuclear strength for defence as well as for deterrence, thus furnishing a sound basis from which to negotiate and underlining that negotiation is the only sensible road open. Progress towards a meaningful detente in an era of negotiation will, therefore, require the maintenance of a strong collective defence posture.

7. The present NATO defence strategy of deterrence and defence, with its constituent concepts of flexibility in response and forward defence, will remain valid. It will continue to require an appropriate mix of nuclear and conventional forces.

8. It is to be hoped that success in strategic arms limitation talks will be achieved. Allied strategic nuclear capability will in any event remain a key element in the security of the West during the 1970s. At the present time, adequate nuclear forces exist and it will be essential to ensure that this capability, which includes the continued commitment of theatre nuclear forces, is maintained.

9. The situation in the field of conventional forces is less satisfactory in view of certain imbalances between NATO and Warsaw Pact capabilities. Careful attention needs to be paid to priorities in improving NATO's conventional strength in the 1970s. In the allocation of resources, priority will be given to measures most critical to a balanced Alliance defence posture in terms of deterrent effect, ability to resist external political pressure, and the prompt availability or rapid enhancement of the forward defensive capability in a developing crisis. In addition to a capability to deter and counter major deliberate aggression, Allied forces should be so structured and organ-

186

ized as to be capable of dealing also with aggressions and incursions with more limited objectives associated with intimidation or the creation of *faits accomplis*, or with those aggressions which might be the result of accident or miscalculation. In short, Allied forces should be so structured and organized as to deter and counter any kind of aggression. Important areas in NATO's conventional defence posture to which attention should be paid in the next decade include: armour/anti-armour potential; the air situation including aircraft protection; overall maritime capabilities, with special reference to anti-submarine forces; the situation on NATO's flanks; the peacetime deployment of ground forces; further improvements in Allied mobilization and reinforcement capabilities as well as in NATO communications, for crisis management purposes.

10. The Alliance possesses the basic resources for adequate conventional strength. However, member countries are confronted with diverging trends in the pattern of expenditures and costs. On the other hand the cost of personnel and equipment continues to mount and most NATO countries are faced with major re-equipment programmes; on the other, in many member countries the share of GNP devoted to defence has declined and, even if outlays in money terms have risen, outlays in real terms have diminished owing to inflation. In marked contrast with the trend in Warsaw Pact countries' military expenditure, defence expenditures of the NATO European countries taken as a whole and calculated in real terms went down by 4% from 1964 to 1969.

11. It is of paramount importance that there be close collaboration among all member states to ensure the most

effective collective defence posture. It is equally important that the burden of maintaining the necessary military strength should be borne co-operatively with each member making an appropriate contribution.

12. The commitment of substantial North American forces deployed in Europe is essential both politically and militarily for effective deterrence and defence and to demonstrate the solidarity of NATO. Their replacement by European forces would be no substitute. At the same time their significance is closely related to an effective and improved European defence effort. Ten of the European countries have therefore consulted among themselves to determine how it would be possible for them individually and collectively to make a more substantial contribution to the overall defence of the Treaty area.

13. As a result the ten countries have decided to adopt a special European Defence Improvement Programme going well beyond previously existing plans and designed to improve Alliance capability in specific fields identified as of particular importance in the current study. This Programme will comprise:

(a) and additional collective contribution, in the order of $420 million over five years, to NATO common infrastructure to accelerate work on the NATO integrated communications system and on aircraft survival measures;

(b) numerous important additions and improvements to national forces, costing at least $450-500 million over the next five years plus very substantial further amounts thereafter; the forces concerned will all be committed to NATO;

(c) other significant financial measures to improve collective defence capability, costing $79 million over the next two years.

The United States and Canada have welcomed this Programme, and have reaffirmed their intention to maintain their forces in Europe at substantially their current levels.

14. After careful review of the proposals emerging from the examination of defence problems in the Seventies, the Defence Planning Committee in Ministerial Session on 2nd December, 1970, adopted concrete proposals aimed at improving NATO's defence capabilities.

DECLARATION ON ATLANTIC RELATIONS

This declaration was approved and published by the North Atlantic Council in Ottawa on 19th June, 1974 and signed by Heads of NATO Governments in Brussels on 26th June, 1974.

The members of the North Atlantic Alliance declare that the Treaty signed 25 years ago to protect their freedom and independence has confirmed their common destiny. Under the shield of the Treaty, the Allies have maintained their security, permitting them to preserve the values which are the heritage of their civilization and enabling Western Europe to rebuild from its ruins and lay the foundations of its unity.

2. The members of the Alliance reaffirm their conviction that the North Atlantic Treaty provides the indispensable basis for their security, thus making possible the pursuit of detente. They welcome the progress that has been achieved on the road towards detente and harmony among nations, and the fact that a conference of 35 countries of Europe and North America is now seeking to lay down guidelines designed to increase security and co-operation in Europe. They believe that until circumstances permit the introduction of general, complete and controlled disarmament, which alone could provide genuine security for all, the ties uniting them must be maintained. The Allies share a common desire to reduce the burden of arms expenditure on their peoples. But states that wish

to preserve peace have never achieved this aim by neglecting their own security.

3. The members of the Alliance reaffirm that their common defence is one and indivisible. An attack on one or more of them in the area of application of the Treaty shall be considered an attack against them all. The common aim is to prevent any attempt by a foreign power to threaten the independence or integrity of a member of the Alliance. Such an attempt would not only put in jeopardy the security of all members of the Alliance but also threaten the foundations of world peace.

4. At the same time they realize that the circumstances affecting their common defence have profoundly changed in the last ten years: the strategic relationship between the United States and the Soviet Union has reached a point of near equilibrium. Consequently, although all the countries of the Alliance remain vulnerable to attack, the nature of the danger to which they are exposed has changed. The Alliance's problems in the defence of Europe have thus assumed a different and more distinct character.

5. However, the essential elements in the situation which gave rise to the Treaty have not changed. While the commitment of all the Allies to the common defence reduces the risk of external aggression, the contribution to the security of the entire Alliance provided by the nuclear forces of the United States based in the United States as well as in Europe and by the presence of North American forces in Europe remains indispensable.

6. Nevertheless, the Alliance must pay careful attention to the dangers to which it is exposed in the European

region, and must adopt all measures necessary to avert them. The European members who provide three-quarters of the conventional strength of the Alliance in Europe, and two of whom possess nuclear forces capable of playing a deterrent role of their own contributing to the overall strengthening of the deterrence of the Alliance, undertake to make the necessary contribution to maintain the common defence at a level capable of deterring and if necessary repelling all actions directed against the independence and territorial integrity of the members of the Alliance.

7. The United States, for its part, reaffirms its determination not to accept any situation which would expose its Allies to external political or military pressure likely to deprive them of their freedom, and states its resolve, together with its Allies, to maintain forces in Europe at the level required to sustain the credibility of the strategy of deterrence and to maintain the capacity to defend the North Atlantic area should deterrence fail.

8. In this connection the member states of the Alliance affirm that as the ultimate purpose of any defence policy is to deny to a potential adversary the objectives he seeks to attain through an armed conflict, all necessary forces would be used for this purpose. Therefore, while reaffirming that a major aim of their policies is to seek agreements that will reduce the risk of war, they also state that such agreements will not limit their freedom to use all forces at their disposal for the common defence in case of attack. Indeed, they are convinced that their determination to do so continues to be the best assurance that war in all its forms will be prevented.

9. All members of the Alliance agree that the continued presence of Canadian and substantial US forces in

Europe plays an irreplaceable role in the defence of North America as well as of Europe. Similarly the substantial forces of the European Allies serve to defend Europe and North America as well. It is also recognized that the further progress towards unity, which the member states of the European Community are determined to make, should in due course have a beneficial effect on the contribution to the common defence of the Alliance of those of them who belong to it. Moreover, the contributions made by members of the Alliance to the preservation of international security and world peace are recognized to be of great importance.

10. The members of the Alliance consider that the will to combine their efforts to ensure their common defence obliges them to maintain and improve the efficiency of their forces and that each should undertake, according to the role that it has assumed in the structure of the Alliance, its proper share of the burden of maintaining the security of all. Conversely, they take the view that in the course of current or future negotiations nothing must be accepted which could diminish this security.

11. The Allies are convinced that the fulfilment of their common aims requires the maintenance of close consultation, co-operation and mutual trust, thus fostering the conditions necessary for defence and favourable for detente, which are complementary. In the spirit of the friendship, equality and solidarity which characterize their relationships, they are firmly resolved to keep each other fully informed and to strengthen the practice of frank and timely consultations by all means which may be appropriate on matters relating to their common interests as members of the Alliance, bearing in mind that these

interests can be affected by events in other areas of the world. They wish also to ensure that their essential security relationship is supported by harmonious political and economic relations. In particular they will work to remove sources of conflict between their economic policies and to encourage economic co-operation with one another.

12. They recall that they have proclaimed their dedication to the principles of democracy, respect for human rights, justice and social progress, which are the fruits of their shared spiritual heritage and they declare their intention to develop and deepen the application of these principles in their countries. Since these principels, by their very nature, forbid any recourse to methods incompatible with the promotion of world peace, they reaffirm that the efforts which they make to preserve their independence, to maintain their security and to improve the living standards of their peoples exclude all forms of aggression against anyone, are not directed against any other country, and are designed to bring about the general improvement of international relations. In Europe, their objective continues to be the pursuit of understanding and co-operation with every European country. In the world at large, each Allied country recognizes the duty to help the developing countries. It is in the interest of all that every country benefit from technical and economic progress in an open and equitable world system.

13. They recognize that the cohesion of the Alliance has found expression not only in co-operation among their governments, but also in the free exchange of views among the elected representatives of the peoples of the Alliance. Accordingly, they declare their support for the strengthening of links among Parliamentarians.

194

14. The members of the Alliance rededicate themselves to the aims and ideals of the North Atlantic Treaty during this year of the twenty-fifth anniversary of its signature. The member nations look to the future, confident that the vitality and creativity of their peoples are commensurate with the challenges which confront them. They declare their conviction that the North Atlantic Alliance continues to serve as an essential element in the lasting structure of peace they are determined to build.

NORTH ATLANTIC COUNCIL

Final Communique

1. The North Atlantic Council met with the participation of Heads of State and Government in Washington
on 30 and 31 May, 1978.

2. Since its inception the Alliance has served to
guarantee security, enhance co-operation and cohesion and
promote peace. Its fundamental vitality lies in the fact
that all Allied countries enjoy democratic systems of
government. The Allies remain convinced that these
systems provide the most humane and effective means
of organizing society to deal with the challenges of the
modern world. They reaffirmed the central rôle of the
Alliance as the guardian of their collective security and
renewed their pledge to consult with one another about the
common goals and purposes of the Alliance for the years
ahead.

3. The Allied leaders noted that their meeting follows
a year of intense activity analysis and reassessment, aimed
at ensuring that the Alliance can meet future tasks. In
particular, the Allies have successfully undertaken the study
and implementation of the decisions and initiatives taken
in common at the Council's meeting in London last May.

4. The fresh study of long-term trends in East-West
relations, decided upon in London, has confirmed the

continuing validity of the two complementary aims of the Alliance, to maintain security and pursue detente. Based on an examination of the situation and trends in the USSR and the other Warsaw Pact countries, the Council's study concludes that members of the Alliance must maintain their solidarity and their vigilance, and keep their defences at the level rendered necessary by the Warsaw Pact's offensive capabilities, while, at the same time, striving to promote détente. The study has also confirmed that relations between the Allies and the Warsaw Pact countries have become more extensive, but that serious causes of tension still persist.

5.   The Allied leaders noted with concern the repeated instances in which the Soviet Union and some of its allies have exploited situations of instability and regional conflict in the developing world. Disregard for the indivisibility of détente cannot but jeopardise the further improvement of East-West relations. They also emphasised, however, that these situations should not be viewed exclusively in an East-West context and reaffirmed the importance they attach to encouraging peaceful settlements through negotation by the countries and regional organizations themselves.

6.   The Allies reviewed the developments concerning Berlin and Germany as a whole. They noted that since the Ministerial Meeting in December 1977, the situation in and around Berlin had been generally without serious disturbance, but that the difficulties had persisted in certain important fields. They reaffirmed the previously stated positions of the Alliance, particularly the conviction that the strict observance and full implementation of all pro-

visions of the Quadripartite Agreement of 3 September, 1971 are essential for the promotion of détente, the maintenance of security and the development of co-operation throughout Europe.

7. The Allies remain determined to pursue as constructive and positive a relationship as possible with the Soviet Union and the other East European countries, which they see as being essential to international peace. They reaffirmed their view that closer contact and understanding should be further encouraged, with a view to enlarging the basis for a more genuine and lasting détente.

8. The Allies remain convinced that full implementation of the CSCE Final Act is of essential importance to the improvement of East-West relations. The Allies welcomed the thorough review of implementation which took place in Belgrade, and noted that human rights and humanitarian questions have been confirmed as legitimate areas of concern to the international community. They recalled that all participating states reaffirmed their resolve to implement the Helsinki Final Act in full and their will to continue the multilateral process initiated by the CSCE. They regretted, however, that the Belgrade meeting did not have a more substantial outcome; they stressed the importance of better implementation of all the provisions of the Final Act so that, by the time of the Madrid meeting in 1980, the review of implementation will show that significant improvement has been made not only in relations between states, but also in the lives of individuals. In this respect, they found it incompatible with the Final Act and with détente that the Soviet Union and some other Eastern European countries fail to recog-

nise the right of their citizens to act upon the provisions of the Helsinki document without being subjected to repressive measures.

9. The Allied leaders reiterated their determination to work vigorously for a more effective and equitable world economic system. The governments of the Allied countries, by their longstanding efforts in extending aid to the developing countries, have demonstrated the importance they attach to this objective. They call upon the Warsaw Pact countries to participate fully in this endeavour.

10. International co-operation in the fields of science and technology and of the environment can likewise contribute to a better world. In this respect, Allied leaders noted with satisfaction the achievements of the **NATO** Science Committee, which recently celebrated its 20th Anniversary, and of the Committee on the Challenges of Modern Society.

11. Having in mind the provisions of Article 2 of the North Atlantic Treaty, the Allied leaders recognise the great importance of securing a sound basis for the further improvement of the economic and social conditions of their peoples. Difficulties in maintaining a sufficient and sustained economic growth are effecting the ability of some members of the Alliance to maintain an effective defence effort. In addition to Allied assistance and co-operation in the defence field, those countries also need economic assistance and co-operation aimed at helping them in their development programmes and in the improvement of the living standards of their peoples. To this end, the Secretary General was invited to conduct a

study, taking into account existing efforts by Allied members bilaterally and in other international fora, and to report to the Council on the way in which this problem could be addressed.

12. The Allies noted with satisfaction the meeting of the Prime Ministers of Greece and Turkey. They expressed the hope that this dialogue on bilateral questions will contribute to the solution of the differences between the two countries.

13. The Allies reaffirmed the importance they attach to the strengthening of cohesion and solidarity especially in the South Eastern flank. They expressed the hope that existing problems will be resolved, and that full co-operation among members of the Alliance in all aspects of the defence field would be resumed.

14. Having considered the situation in the Middle East, the Allied leaders expressed the hope that efforts aiming at a comprehensive settlement in the area would continue. They urged all parties concerned to redouble their efforts to reach a just and lasting peace.

15. The efforts by the Allies to reduce tensions between East and West and to discourage attempts to use military power for political ends, can only be successfully pursued in the context of a stable military balance. Such a balance would ensure that they can pursue their détente policies in safety and with confidence.

16. The Allied leaders expressed their concern at the continual expansion of Warsaw Pact offensive capabilities. Faced with this situation, and notwithstanding Soviet state-

ments that these massive military resources are not designed to threaten the security of the Allied countries, the latter have no option but to continue two complementary approaches: on the one hand, strengthen their defensive capabilities and on the other, seek to promote negotiations on arms control and disarmament agreements. The Allies will continue to follow the latter approach whenever possible, but progress in this direction necessarily depends on a positive attitude on the part of the Warsaw Pact countries.

17. The Allied leaders recognised that effective and verifiable limitation of arms, aimed in particular at correcting the existing imbalances in Europe in the conventional field, is an indispensable condition for a durable improvement in East-West relations and for the consolidation of peace.

18. The Allied leaders discussed the US-USSR Strategic Arms Limitation Talks. They welcomed progress made in the negotiations and expressed support for US efforts to conclude an agreement which is responsive to the security interests and concerns of the Alliance and which enhances strategic stability and maintains deterrence.

19. With respect to Mutual and Balanced Force Reductions, the Allies who participate in the negotiations in Vienna reaffirmed their commitment to these negotiations which they first proposed at the Ministerial Meeting in Reykjavik ten years ago, and their determination to bring them to a successful conclusion. They confirmed their endorsement of the agreed objective of the negotiations to contribute to a more stable relationship and the strengthening of peace and security in Europe. This objective

would be achieved by their proposal to create approximate parity in ground forces in the area of reductions through the establishment of a common collective ceiling on ground force manpower and the reduction of the disparity in tanks.

They called attention to the important new initiative which they introduced into the negotiations on 19 April, to which they now look for a serious and constructive response from the Warsaw Pact participants. These Allies consider that the data discussion in Vienna is an essential element in the efforts towards a satisfactory outcome and that the clarification of the data base is therefore decisive for substantial progress in the negotiations.

These Allies state that they will propose that a meeting of the negotiations at Foreign Minister level should be convened at an appropriate date once substantial progress has been made in the negotiations and it is clear that a meeting at this level could contribute effectively to the early conclusion of a mutually satisfactory agreement.

20. The Allies welcomed the United Nations Special Session on Disarmament. They expressed their resolve to participate in it constructively and their hope that this important conference would produce substantial results. Allied leaders agreed that the destructiveness of modern weaponry, the danger of the proliferation of nuclear weapons, the needs of the developing countries and the requirements of their own societies make co-operation on a wide range of disarmament and arms control issues an urgent task for all countries. Progress in this direction cannot but contribute to international prosperity and make easier the necessary growth in financial resources devoted to development. The Allies reaffirmed their determination to persevere, through negotiation, in the pursuit of realistic and verifiable disarmament and arms control

measures that enhance stability, reduce force levels and promote security. To these ends, they agreed to make fuller use of the Alliance machinery for thorough consultation on arms control and disarmament issues.

21. Until such time as it proves possible to achieve a satisfactory military balance at lower levels of forces through realistic and verifiable force reduction agreements, the Allies will continue to devote all these resources necessary to modernize and strengthen their own forces to the extent required for deterrence and defence. They will continue the efforts they have undertaken to preserve and promote the strong industrial and technical capability which is essential to the defence of the Alliance as a whole. The provision of new and existing generations of weaponry will require the most effective use of defence resources and deepened co-operation in armaments. In this connection, the Allies welcomed the steps that had been taken pursuant to the initiative agreed in London on the intensification of the Transatlantic Dialogue. The Allies are convinced that the effectiveness of their forces can be increased through enhanced interoperability and standardization of equipment and defence equipment planning procedures.

22. Against the background of the study of long-term trends in East-West relations and other matters affecting Western security, leaders of states taking part in the integrated defence structure of the Alliance considered on 31 May a report on the Long-Term Defence Programme prepared by their Defence Ministers, which had been commissioned at the London Summit Meeting in May 1977.

23. They noted with approval that emphasis was placed in the Long-Term Defence Programme on greater

co-operative efforts and on the need for NATO co-ordinated defence planning to be projected into the longer term. The leaders of these states endorsed specific programmes approved by Defence Ministers to improve the readiness of NATO's forcs and the mobilization of reserves, to strengthen NATO's air defences, to counter the electronic warfare threat, to enhance NATO's maritime posture, to provide more effective logistic support for all NATO forces, and to improve NATO's command, control and communications arrangements. They approved programmes designed to accelerate the movement of significant reinforcements to the forward areas in a time of crisis, envisaging the commitment of civil air, sea, land and national infrastructure resources; and they welcomed in particular the United States intention to preposition heavy equipment for three additional United States divisions in the Central Region of Allied Command Europe by 1982, recognising the need for European Allies to provide the necessary support and other facilities. They also noted with interest the work underway in the Nuclear Planning Group towards meeting needs for the modernization of theatre nuclear forces.

24. These Allied leaders noted with satisfaction that almost all countries had indicated their intention to adjust their financial plans for defence in accordance with the aim, established in the 1977 Ministerial Guidance, of an annual increase in defence expenditure in the region of 3% in real terms. They also stressed the importance of achieving the most effective return from resources made available or planned for defence by the achievement of a greater degree of co-operation and rationalization; they welcomed the emphasis placed in the Long-Term Defence Programme on this objective.

25. They expressed their support for the Long-Term Defence Programme forwarded by their Defence Ministers, as a major contribution towards adapting NATO's forces to the changing needs of the 1980s. They called for vigorous follow-through action to be taken by national authorities and at NATO and international military headquarters. In this connection, Turkey pointed out the importance to her participation of sufficient support from her Allies as well as of the complete removal of existing restrictions on the procurement of defence equipment.

26. In taking these decisions, these Allied leaders concluded that, in the absence of equitable arms control and disarmament agreements, a satisfactory balance in strategic, theatre nuclear and conventional terms could only be assured by greater efforts to modernize and strengthen the military capacity of the Alliance. They stressed that the maintenance of security is indispensable for the continued freedom, individual liberty and welfare of their societies and for the furthering of détente.

Maria Rita Saulle is Professor of the History of Treaties and International Policy on the Faculty of Law at the University of Rome. Prior of this Prof. Saulle was responsible for the Faculty course on International Law.

Prof. Saulle is a Member of the International Law Association and of the American Society of International Law and she collaborated for many years with the International Institute for the Unification of Private Law (UNIDROIT).

Prof. Saulle's publications include: *L'errore negli atti giuridici internazionali*, Milan 1963; *Le avarie comuni nel diritto internazionale privato marittimo e aeronautico*, Milan 1970; *Appunti di storia e di diritto dei Trattati*, Rome 1977, besides many articles and notes.